Fiscal Management in
Resource-Rich Countries

A WORLD BANK STUDY

Fiscal Management in Resource-Rich Countries

Essentials for Economists, Public Finance Professionals, and Policy Makers

Rolando Ossowski and Håvard Halland

WORLD BANK GROUP

Contents

Boxes

Figures

Tables

Acknowledgments

This volume, the second of the two-volume publication *Essentials for Economists, Public Finance Professionals, and Policy Makers*, published in the World Bank Studies series, was prepared by Rolando Ossowski, consultant to the World Bank, as the primary author, and Håvard Halland, economist at the World Bank. Its production was led by Håvard Halland. The volume draws on a large number of World Bank, International Monetary Fund (IMF), and publicly available documents. The text also draws heavily on, and includes material from, Davis, Ossowski, and Fedelino (2003); Ossowski (2013a, 2013b); and Villafuerte, López-Murphy, and Ossowski (2010). Ossowski and others (2008); In particular, Ossowski (2013b) drew on an earlier draft of this work, and substantial material from that publication is included in this volume. The objective of this volume is not to present original research, nor to represent a World Bank position, but rather to survey and summarize insights from an extensive body of literature, and condense these insights into an easily readable format.

The authors are grateful to the Governance Partnership Facility and its donor partners—the U.K. Department for International Development (DFID), the Australian Department of Foreign Affairs and Trade (DFAT), the Netherlands' Ministry of Foreign Affairs, and Norway's Ministry of Foreign Affairs—for providing full funding for this work. The authors wish to thank Albert Zeufack, Enrique Blanco Armas, R. Sudharshan Canagarah, and Yue Man Lee for excellent peer review comments and suggestions that significantly improved the quality of the final product. William Dorotinsky, Adrian Fozzard, Silvana Tordo, and Marijn Verhoeven provided highly useful feedback on earlier drafts. The authors would also like to thank Robert Beschel and Nicola Smithers for their support of this work. Importantly, the accuracy of country-specific information was strengthened by essential feedback from numerous colleagues in World Bank country offices around the world. The authors are grateful for their detailed reviews of previous drafts. Alberto Gonzales provided excellent assistance with the data. Editorial work by Fayre Makeig made the study much easier to read. Copyrights for tables and figures drawn from other sources were obtained by Catherine Lips.

The authors are grateful to the IMF for generously granting usage rights for copyrighted figures. All opinions, errors, and omissions are the authors' own.

About the Authors

Rolando Ossowski is an economic consultant to the World Bank. He is a former staff member of the International Monetary Fund (IMF), where he held a number of positions, including that of assistant director in the Fiscal Affairs Department. He holds a PhD in economics from the London School of Economics. His major interests are macroeconomics, public finance, and fiscal management issues in resource-rich countries. He is author or joint author of research papers, book chapters, and IMF occasional papers. He is coeditor of *Fiscal Policy Formulation and Implementation in Oil-Producing Countries*, published by the IMF (2003). He has given presentations at many international conferences and seminars.

Håvard Halland is a senior economist at the World Bank. His research and advisory work has focused on the economics and finance of the extractive industries sector. Research and policy agendas include resource-backed infrastructure finance, sovereign wealth fund policy, extractive industries revenue management, and fiscal management in resource-rich countries. He is an author or joint author of academic and policy papers, book chapters, magazine articles, and blogs. He regularly gives presentations at international conferences and seminars. Before joining the World Bank, he was a delegate and program manager for the International Committee of the Red Cross in the Democratic Republic of the Congo and Colombia. He earned a PhD in economics from the University of Cambridge.

Overview

What Should We Know about the Extractive Industries Sector?

Economists and public finance professionals working in resource-rich countries are frequently confronted with issues that require an in-depth understanding of the extractive industries (EI) sector, its economics, governance, and policy challenges, as well as the implications of natural resource wealth for fiscal and public financial management (PFM). The objective of the two-volume *Essentials for Economists, Public Finance Professionals, and Policy Makers*, published in the World Bank Studies series, is to provide a concise overview of the extractive-related topics that economists, public finance professionals, and policy makers are likely to encounter. Volume I, *The Extractive Industries Sector* (Halland, Lokanc, and Nair 2015), provides an introduction to the sector, including an overview of issues core to its economics, institutional framework, project and investment cycles, and contract management, and a description of the components of sector governance and policy. Volume II, *Fiscal Management in Resource-Rich Countries*, addresses the fiscal challenges typically encountered when managing large revenue flows from the EI sector. Since oil and mineral taxation, including subnational revenue sharing, has been extensively addressed elsewhere, the *Essentials* provide only brief treatment of this topic, while referring the reader to relevant sources.

This initial overview provides a common introduction to the two volumes. To this end, it first outlines several key characteristics and challenges that distinguish the EI sector from other sectors. It then reviews experiences of countries that have undertaken successful extractive-led development, and it synthesizes key findings from literature on the so-called resource curse hypothesis (which argues that countries rich in oil and minerals have lower growth and worse development outcomes than their peers). It concludes by introducing the two volumes in turn.

How Does the Extractive Industries Sector Differ from Other Sectors?

The EI sector occupies an outsize space in the economies of many resource-rich countries. Specifically, it accounts for at least 20 percent of total exports, and at least 20 percent of government revenue, in 29 low-income and lower-middle-income countries. In eight such countries, the EI sector accounts for more than 90 percent of total exports and 60 percent of total government revenue (IMF 2012a). Meanwhile, the expansion of the extractive sector has spurred investment in these countries, reflected in the quintupling of foreign direct investment in Africa between 2000 and 2012—from $10 billion to $50 billion (UNCTAD 2013).

In principle, the extractive sector is not necessarily more complex than other economic sectors. Companies make holes in the ground from which they extract oil, gas, or minerals to be transported to a processing facility in-country or to an export point. Conveniently, the extracted commodities can be weighed and their quality measured, prices of common commodities are quoted on international exchanges, and the industry is dominated by a tiny number of very large companies (Calder 2014). Nevertheless, the economic, societal, and environmental implications of EI operations pose significant and diverse challenges.

For companies, the exploration and extraction of oil, gas, and minerals involve high levels of geological uncertainty, large initial capital investments, and long exploration and project development periods. The high volatility of oil and mineral prices and the unpredictability of costs generate price and cost risks. EI projects may also generate high risks to the natural environment. The costs of decommissioning projects and, in some cases, the cleanup of contaminated soil or water, can constitute a significant part of total project costs; companies will typically be required to post collateral to ensure that funding is available to responsibly decommission the project at the end of its operative life. If not taken into account during the licensing of extraction rights, environmental costs could end up as government liabilities instead of on the company balance sheet. Local-level considerations also include the socioeconomic circumstances and health of populations living in the vicinity of the extractive project. To mitigate potentially adverse social and environmental impacts, and ensure that a share of benefits accrues to affected populations, resource companies may be required to meet specific commitments through community development agreements and community foundations, trusts, and funds.

For governments, the exhaustible, nonrenewable character of oil, gas, and mineral resources poses challenges relevant to the determination of optimal extraction rates; the design of the fiscal regime; and the allocation of resource revenues to investment, consumption, and foreign savings. The exhaustibility of subsoil resources also raises complex questions around intergenerational equity and long-term fiscal sustainability. Fiscal planning is likely to be significantly affected by the time profile of extraction and by expected and actual commodity prices.

In the EI sector, specialized technology and high capital requirements generate barriers to entry. As a result, the sector is dominated by large multinational firms with vertically integrated value chains and specialized intellectual property. In low-income countries, this usually means that high-value machines and equipment for operations are imported, whereas the natural resources they extract are exported. The complexity of large-scale multinational operations requires resource-rich countries to develop adequate institutional capacity to establish and operate efficient contracting, legal, and fiscal regimes and to oversee company operations. At the other end of the spectrum, small-scale artisanal mining may provide livelihoods for low-income families, but extensive use of toxic chemicals could result in large liabilities for the government if it must pick up the tab for cleanup.

The locations of natural resource extraction sites are predetermined by geography; extraction projects (unlike manufacturing, for example) cannot be shifted to less costly locations. The global production value chain, meanwhile, involves complex organizational and financing structures that may take advantage of tax treaties and innovative financing mechanisms to ensure that transactions are tax efficient. From the perspective of public revenue management, the global value chain implies challenges related to transfer pricing and beneficial ownership.[1]

The extractive sector is characterized by exceptional profits—and substantial rents, defined as the difference between production costs (including "normal" profits) and revenue from sales. The rents can be highly volatile, as they respond to fluctuations in commodity prices and extraction costs, presenting further challenges to the design of fiscal regimes. Resource prices not only fluctuate to extremes, but they do so unpredictably. The fact that countries' resource revenues are typically generated by exports, in the form of foreign currency inflows, puts pressure on exchange rates, with potentially significant effects on competitiveness and macroeconomic stability.

The EI sector, more than many others, depends for its efficient functioning on a complex ecosystem of governmental institutions and functions. The establishment of a fertile EI investment climate requires not only good and well-implemented legal and regulatory regimes but also a functional geodata information base and a mineral rights cadastre. The multifaceted character of the sector is reflected by the involvement of a large number of ministries and public entities whose coordination may be highly complex. Efficient extractive-based economic development requires the effective cooperation of these public entities while drawing on the specialized capacity of each. Yet, cooperation often suffers as individual entities seek to maintain control of their share of the extractive portfolio—and revenues.

Although there is no single explanation for the resource curse, many elements of successful natural-resource-based growth are by now relatively well understood. Countries that have benefited from the EI sector tend to have embraced policies with a common set of characteristics: efficient fiscal regimes and macroeconomic stabilization; the conscientious development of specialized public management capacity in the oil, gas, and mining sectors; and productive investments in infrastructure, human development, and economic diversification. These countries' sustainable and equitable long-term growth has resulted from investing resource revenues in durable assets, as well as from coordinating diverse economic sectors toward the common goal of resource-based growth. Hence, to optimize the monetary and nonmonetary benefits of oil, gas, and mineral extraction, EI sector policies need to go beyond individual project to consider and address the complex set of capabilities needed to ensure the sector's efficient operation and its delivery of optimal benefits to both citizens and the government.

The Blessing, and Curse, of Resource Abundance

Some resource-rich countries have succeeded in converting resource wealth into long-term and equitable economic development, while many others have not. Natural resources have played a fundamental role in the growth of several industrialized economies, including Germany and the United Kingdom, where coal and iron ore deposits were a precondition for the Industrial Revolution. The United States was the world's leading mineral economy from the mid-nineteenth to the mid-twentieth century and in the same period became the world's leader in manufacturing (van der Ploeg 2011). More recently, countries such as Botswana, Chile, and Norway have used abundant oil and mineral resources as the foundation for economic growth. However, in many other countries, resource extraction appears to have undermined governance, fed corruption and capital flight, and increased inequality.

Why do some countries succeed in leveraging their natural resources, while others have low growth performance in spite of immense subsoil wealth? This question has been the subject of extensive debate. Sachs and Warner (1995) confirmed a negative relationship between the extractive export share of gross domestic product (GDP) and economic growth. They concluded that resource abundance is associated with slower growth, a relationship that was later labeled the "resource curse." Other authors, using different methods, have disputed the existence of a universal resource curse (Alexeev and Conrad 2009). Brunnschweiler and Bulte 2006; Davis and Tilton 2005; While the existence of such a curse is certainly disputable, it is nevertheless clear that a number of resource-rich developing countries, in spite of growth spikes during periods of particularly high oil and mineral prices, have not been able to translate resource wealth into sustainable long-term growth. As Davis and Tilton (2005, 233) put it:

> While [the question of] whether or not mining usually promotes economic development remains unresolved, there is widespread agreement that rich mineral deposits provide developing countries with opportunities, which in some instances have been used wisely to promote development, and in other instances have been misused, hurting development. The consensus on this issue is important, for it means that one uniform policy toward all mining in the developing world is not desirable ... The appropriate public policy question is not should we or should we not promote mining in the developing countries, but rather where should we encourage it and how can we ensure that it contributes as much as possible to economic development and poverty alleviation.

Although a full review of the literature on the resource curse is beyond the scope of this work, a summary of its main arguments provides useful background. Much of the literature subsequent to Sachs and Warner (1995) concentrates on identifying the mechanisms by which natural resources affect growth. The relative importance of such mechanisms has been much debated and remains the subject of substantive disagreement.

The culprits most often blamed for the resource curse include "Dutch disease," low or inefficient investment (including in human capital), fiscal indiscipline and high consumption, the decay of institutions, and output volatility generated by volatility of oil and mineral prices. The so-called Dutch disease is often cited. The name alludes to the appreciation of the Dutch currency following oil production in the North Sea in the 1960s and refers to the dynamics by which high production in the extractive sector generates increased demand in the nontradable (services) sector and thus causes the currency to appreciate. This appreciation, in turn, leads to reduced exports from the nonextractive tradable sector (Corden and Neary 1982), which may negatively affect growth.

Institutional quality, as reflected in the rule of law and in the quality of public sector management, is frequently referred to as a possible cause of the resource curse. Political economists point out that in many countries that have found it difficult to generate resource-based growth, the discovery of oil, gas, or minerals was preceded by a legacy of poor governance and weak institutions. Weak institutions offer few checks on rent seeking and corruption. While a small elite may become extremely rich off resource rents, the population as a whole receives few benefits. Mehlum, Moene, and Torvik (2006), for example, distinguish between institutional contexts that are "grabber friendly" and those that are "producer friendly." "Grabbers" of resource revenues are more likely to have free rein where institutions are weak. If serving in a government position is seen as a way to get rich quick, instances of "grabbing" may accelerate. Political economists point out that where incumbent politicians fear removal from office, the administration is likely to extract faster than the socially optimal rate and will borrow against future resource revenues. Common phenomena in such contexts may include capital flight, high private consumption among those in power, and high rates of public spending to benefit favored clients (van der Ploeg 2011). Incumbents who fear losing office may also avoid accumulating public savings—for example, in a sovereign wealth fund (SWF)—that could be raided by a future government, preferring instead to overinvest in partisan projects that increase their own hold on power.

While institutional strength may determine the success of extractive-based development, large revenue flows from the EI sector may degrade institutions. Where large revenue flows occur amid insecure property rights, poorly functioning legal systems, and imperfect markets, they are likely to prompt rent seeking (Torvik 2002). Resource revenues increase the value of being in power. Where they provide funding for autocratic regimes, they can in effect prevent the redistribution of political power to the middle class, thereby impeding the adoption of growth-promoting policies (Bourguignon and Verdier 2000). In the same vein, the availability of such revenues may encourage elites to block technological and institutional improvements that could weaken their hold on power (Acemoğlu and Robinson 2006). In the extreme, disputes over access to natural resources may spark armed conflict. Collier and Hoeffler (2004) estimate that a country whose natural resources compose more than 25 percent of GDP faces a 23 percent probability of civil conflict—against 0.5 percent for a country with no resources.

It can be argued that the political economy literature and its application of economic modeling to the resource sector have substantial weaknesses. Weaknesses of the existing theory include the following:

The property right over the resource is assumed to be held by the state, and rents flow from the ground without need of investment or effort.

Despite the models having a purported focus on subsoil resources, they all ignore the finite nature of these resources. No consideration is given to stock constraints; many models simply assume an infinite resource, produced without any effort or costs. None of the approaches explicitly models a mineral, gas, or oil resource.

Although state ownership of natural resources is a feature observed in many countries, the models fail to examine the sensitivity of outcomes to different property rights arrangements (for example, private ownership with taxation, some direct state participation, and indigenization policies).

Resource abundance may exacerbate fiscal indiscipline. Sudden revenue windfalls from extractives tend to generate expectations of increased public expenditure, which may prompt the excessive loosening of fiscal policy, and low savings. The result can be public investment in unnecessary or unproductive project and increased sovereign debt. Whereas observed and optimal savings rates seem to differ little in nonresource economies, they differ sharply in resource-rich countries (van der Ploeg 2011). Bleaney and Halland (2016) do not find evidence that natural resource wealth in general promotes fiscal indiscipline. In fact, their results indicate that fuel exporters tend to have a better general government fiscal balance. However, some of the resource-rich countries in their sample have, after oil or mineral discoveries, exhibited severe fiscal indiscipline that cannot be explained by the authors' econometric model. Findings from other papers testify to the importance of early management of expectations, real fiscal discipline as opposed to a reliance on fiscal rules, full and real (as opposed to nominal) independence of the central bank, as well as the establishment of means to isolate from political pressures the SWF and the government entity responsible for oil revenue projection.

If the volatility of commodity prices—and in turn of public revenue flows from extractives—is passed on to public expenditures and output, it may have a damaging effect on growth. Van der Ploeg and Poelhekke (2010) find that natural resource wealth has a positive direct effect on growth, which is more or less canceled out by the indirect effect of output volatility. In this line of argument, the resource curse would arise from the high volatility of commodity prices, with an effect on growth via output volatility that may be mitigated by financial sector development and openness to trade. Bleaney and Halland (2014) find that the volatility of public expenditure—alongside overall institutional quality—explains slower growth, indicating that resource-rich countries that are able to smooth public expenditures do better than their peers.

Unless there is technology transfer from the EI sector to national industries, resource wealth could contribute to deindustrialization. Yet, some resource-rich countries have achieved broad industrial development even as their currency has appreciated amid large resource exports. Dutch disease thus fails to fully explain the different industrial development trajectories observed across resource-rich countries. Some studies (Gylfason, Herbertsson, and Zoega 1999; Matsuyama 1992) suggest that resource-based industrialization and growth take place if the extractive sector is a source of technology transfer and "learning by doing." Torvik (2001) points to Norway as an example: here, according to his argument, natural resource extraction prompted learning by doing in both the traded and nontraded sectors.

For more complete surveys of the resource curse literature, interested readers are referred to Frankel (2010) and van der Ploeg (2011).

Content of the Two Volumes

The first volume, *The Extractive Industries Sector*, provides an overview of issues core to EI economics; discusses key components of the sector's governance, policy, and institutional frameworks; and identifies the public sector's EI-related financing obligations. Its discussion of EI economics covers the valuation of subsoil assets, the economic interpretation of ore, and the structure of energy and mineral markets. The volume maps the responsibilities of relevant government entities and outlines the characteristics of the EI sector's legal and regulatory frameworks. Specific key functions of the sector are briefly discussed, such as the administration of geodata and cadastre, the characteristics and administration of an efficient EI fiscal regime, contract management and monitoring, and typical requirements for a fertile EI business environment.

The volume also describes the economic and financial structures that underpin environmental and social safeguards, such as the use of financial sureties for decommissioning, and of community foundations, trusts, and funds. The investment of public revenues generated from oil, gas, or minerals is briefly addressed, with a focus on infrastructure, and there is a short discussion of extractive-based economic diversification and local content development. For interested readers, more specialized publications targeting individual subject areas are sometimes referred to in the first paragraph of the chapters. The interested reader will also find additional material in the appendices, including on revenue collection, revenue projection, and management of contingent liabilities, as well as material on resource classification systems, reserve reporting standards, types of economic rents characteristic of the EI sector, the relationship between fiscal policy and economic reserves, and the impact of income changes on commodity demand.

This second volume, *Fiscal Management in Resource-Rich Countries*, addresses the critical challenges that volatile, uncertain, and exhaustible revenues from the EI sector pose to fiscal policies in these countries. The volume discusses fiscal policy across four related dimensions: policies for short-run stabilization; the management of fiscal risks and vulnerabilities; the promotion of long-term sustainability; and the importance of good PFM,[2] public investment systems, and fiscal transparency. Institutional mechanisms used to help fiscal management are examined, including medium-term expenditure frameworks, fiscal rules, fiscal councils, and resource funds. The volume also discusses revenue earmarking and the resource prices used in the government budget, and it outlines important fiscal indicators for resource-rich countries.

Given the diversity of experiences in resource-rich countries, the topics discussed in the two volumes will be more relevant to some countries than others. Each volume can be read independent of the other, though they address common themes. It is hoped that the information they provide will prove a sound basis for economists, public finance professionals, and policy makers wishing to strengthen the management of the EI sector, and associated fiscal and PFM systems, in their countries.

Notes

1. The IMF's 2014 draft update of the Resource Revenue Management pillar (Pillar IV) of the Fiscal Transparency Code defines a beneficial owner as "the legal entity, or if applicable, the natural person which owns the ultimate economic interest in the holder of a natural resource right within a country, usually through a chain of related parties which may be held in different jurisdictions" (http://www.imf.org/external/np/exr/consult/2014/ftc/pdf/121814.pdf). In the context of tax evasion, corporations may hide their beneficial ownership of one or more related companies so as to avoid scrutiny of alleged arm's-length flows of goods and services between the related companies, or subsidiaries. A beneficial owner of a natural resource would be the legal entity or natural person that owns the holder of extraction rights in a country, potentially via related parties located in different jurisdictions.

2. Subsequent work on PFM, as relevant to natural resources, is in progress.

Abbreviations

ABFA	annual budget funding amount (Ghana)
AHSTF	Alberta's Heritage Savings Trust Fund
bbl	barrel of oil
CAB	cyclically adjusted balance
CEMAC	Central African Economic and Monetary Community
CFAF	Communauté Financière Africaine Franc
CPI	consumer price index
DFA	domestic financial asset
DFAT	Australian Department of Foreign Affairs and Trade
DFID	U.K. Department for International Development
DSA	debt-sustainability analysis
ECA	excess crude account (Nigeria)
EI	extractive industries
ESI	estimated sustainable income (Timor-Leste)
FIV	Fondo de Inversiones de Venezuela
FSDEA	Fundo Soberano de Angola
FSF	fiscal sustainability framework
FSL	fiscal stability law (Mongolia)
FSRG	Fonds Souverain de la République Gabonaise
FY	fiscal year
GAPP	generally accepted principles and practices
GBR	gross borrowing requirement
GDP	gross domestic product
GPF-G	Government Pension Fund-Global (Norway)
IDB	Inter-American Development Bank
IMF	International Monetary Fund
IWGS	International Working Group of Sovereign Wealth Funds
LIC	low-income country
MEC	mining-exporting countries

MENA	Middle East and North Africa
MoF	Ministry of Finance
MTBF	medium-term budget framework
MTEF	medium-term expenditure framework
MTF	medium-term framework
MTFF	medium-term fiscal framework
MTPF	medium-term performance framework
NBIM	Norges Bank Investment Management (Norway)
NDFI	National Development Fund of Iran
NRB	nonresource balance
NRGDP	nonresource GDP
NROG	nonresource output gap
NRPB	nonresource primary balance
OEC	oil-exporting countries
PEMEX	Petróleos Mexicanos
PFM	public financial management
PIH	permanent income hypothesis
PIM	public investment management
PPP	public–private partnerships
PRMA	Petroleum Revenue Management Act (Ghana)
SB	structural balance
SIA	sustainable investing approach
SIF	strategic investment fund
SNG	subnational government
SOE	state-owned enterprise
SPV	special purpose vehicle
SWF	sovereign wealth fund
VaR	value-at-risk
VAT	value added tax
WEO	World Economic Outlook (IMF)
WTI	West Texas Intermediate

Introduction

This volume discusses key fiscal management issues in resource-rich countries and provides suggestions to enhance fiscal management. Countries with large nonrenewable resources can benefit substantially from them, and many countries have done so. But reliance on nonrenewable resource revenue poses significant challenges to policy makers, and the government has an important role to play in how the revenues from these resources are used.

Fiscal policy in resource-rich countries has the same broad objectives as fiscal policy in other countries. It should contribute to the achievement of macroeconomic stability and sustainable and inclusive growth and poverty reduction, within a framework of fiscal sustainability. But while the objectives of fiscal policy in resource-rich countries are similar to those in other countries, dependence on fiscal resource revenue raises a number of specific issues for fiscal policy that require the adaptation of fiscal frameworks to incorporate the special characteristics of these revenues.

This volume focuses on fiscal management in the context of the challenges posed by reliance on resource revenues. It sets out general principles of good fiscal management and tries to suggest paths forward for resource-rich countries where fiscal management is in need of improvement, and sound fiscal principles for new producers. While the volume does not fully answer questions about the sequencing of reforms in the existing fiscal management frameworks in specific developing resource-rich countries—since answers depend on particular country circumstances—it does discuss possible approaches. These include gradual reform, as when first-best solutions are not viable because of capacity constraints, or political or other reasons. The volume tries to condense a large amount of material into a succinct exposition and discussion of the issues, with evidence drawn from international experience and country examples, and provides references for those interested in delving deeper into specific topics.

The volume discusses key elements of fiscal frameworks for resource-rich countries. They include: fiscal strategies to deal with short-term resource-related volatility and uncertainty and to manage resource-related fiscal risks; frameworks for the analysis of fiscal sustainability in the presence of nonrenewable resources; and public financial management (PFM) and public investment management (PIM) systems to enhance the quality of spending. In many resource-rich countries, fiscal frameworks include special fiscal mechanisms and institutions to help fiscal management, and the volume discusses the most important ones, including fiscal rules and resource funds. The volume also includes a detailed discussion of fiscal indicators for resource-rich countries.

The rest of the volume is structured in three parts, which cover: (i) why resource revenue complicates fiscal management; (ii) what fiscal policy can do to address those challenges and foster sustainable growth; and (iii) specific fiscal mechanisms and institutions that some resource-rich countries have used to aid fiscal management.

Part I provides a brief overview of why resource revenue can complicate fiscal management in resource-rich countries. Chapter 1 discusses the main challenges posed by resource revenues. They arise from (i) the volatility and uncertainty of resource revenues, which can complicate fiscal planning and the efficient use of resources; (ii) the dependence of these revenues on the exploitation of depletable natural resources, which gives rise to issues of how much to consume and how much to save; (iii) the fact that the domestic use of revenues that largely originate from abroad can have implications for macroeconomic stability and competitiveness; and (iv) the resource rents that can be associated with natural resources, which can give rise to complications related to the political economy and the quality of public expenditure.

Part II focuses on ways in which fiscal policy can address the challenges posed by resource revenue and foster sustainable growth. The discussion focuses on four broad topics:

- *Fiscal policy and short-run stabilization* (chapter 2). A recurrent challenge for resource-rich countries has been how to manage the impact of volatile and uncertain resource revenues on macroeconomic and financial stability. This is a key issue for development because macroeconomic volatility and uncertainty have adverse effects for long-term growth, poverty reduction, and income distribution. This chapter sets out the macroeconomic, fiscal, and PFM arguments for smoothing government expenditure, thereby contributing to macroeconomic stability and sustainable growth.
- *The management of fiscal risks and vulnerabilities* (chapter 3). Fiscal policy in resource-rich countries must take into account the large volatility and uncertainty of resource revenues. Yet in some resource-rich countries, short-term horizons in annual budgets and lack of adequate risk analysis do not give sufficient weight to resource revenue risks in the medium term, and sometimes not even in the short term. Excessive risk taking can result in the need for costly adjustments when resource prices fall. Fiscal risk analysis is required for the evaluation of proposed spending paths in the medium term—how resilient are they to potential shocks? What buffers can be created to protect public spending in the short run in case of resource revenue downturns? The chapter also discusses, briefly, the management of specific fiscal risks.
- *Promoting sustainability* (chapter 4). Nonrenewable resources are exhaustible and run the risk of obsolescence. Therefore, countries have to consider how to

allocate finite resource wealth to the current generation and to future generations. This has implications for decisions on how much to consume and to save during the period of resource production, and how to allocate savings into different forms of assets. This chapter discusses approaches to fiscal sustainability analysis in resource-rich countries.

- *Public financial management (PFM), public investment management (PIM), and fiscal transparency* (chapter 5). The quality of public expenditure and, in particular, the productivity of public investment are key determinants of the extent to which resource wealth can be turned into other productive assets that foster sustainable growth, development, and poverty reduction. Fiscal transparency and accountability are vital for establishing and preserving credibility in the management of resource revenues and enhancing efficiency and effectiveness in the allocation of resources.

Part III discusses special fiscal institutions and mechanisms that some resource-rich countries have put in place as part of their fiscal frameworks to help fiscal management, and distills lessons and suggestions from conceptual considerations and country experience. It focuses on medium-term expenditure frameworks (MTEFs), fiscal rules and fiscal councils, and resource funds. It clarifies the objectives that might be pursued through the implementation of such mechanisms, the preconditions required for successful implementation, and design and implementation issues, in each case providing some suggestions. It also discusses two other issues: revenue earmarking in resource-rich countries, and the resource prices or revenues used in annual budgets.

- *Medium-term expenditure frameworks* (chapter 6). A medium-term perspective on annual budgeting is essential in any country, and the specific characteristics of resource revenues make the need to link annual budgets to medium- and long-term fiscal objectives particularly important in resource-rich countries. Medium-term frameworks (MTFs) can be designed to help quantify and address fiscal risks, and foster long-term perspectives on fiscal policy.
- *Fiscal rules and fiscal councils* (chapter 7). Fiscal rules are defined as standing commitments to specified numerical targets or ceilings for some key budgetary aggregates. In resource-rich countries, fiscal rules are often motivated by the desire to reduce the procyclicality of fiscal policy in the face of volatile resource revenue, and to promote savings and sustainability. But in these countries, the design of appropriate fiscal rules is more challenging than in other countries, due to the special characteristics of resource revenue. The chapter discusses various designs for fiscal rules; the trade-offs between rigidity and flexibility; and the PFM prerequisites for the effective implementation of fiscal rules. Some countries have set up fiscal councils to reduce fiscal deficit biases and promote transparency. The chapter also provides a brief discussion of fiscal councils in resource-rich countries, and desirable prerequisites to establishing them.

- *Resource funds* (chapter 8). Many resource-rich countries have established re-source funds in response to the challenges and complications that resource revenue poses to fiscal policy and public asset management. Resource funds, as a group, form part of a wider set of funds known as sovereign wealth funds (SWFs). The chapter discusses resource fund objectives and design and im-plementation issues, and provides an extended discussion of the issues raised by funds with authority to invest or spend domestically. It also discusses issues of design consistency when the country's fiscal framework includes both fiscal rules and resource funds.
- *Revenue earmarking* (chapter 9). Some resource-rich countries have assigned shares of revenue from certain specified taxes or from general budget revenue to specific expenditures or to broad expenditure areas, whether through law or constitutional clauses. The motivations for earmarking include the desire to improve resource allocation, to ensure the funding of vulnerable expenditure categories, to protect temporary revenues and assign them to appropriate uses, and generally to prevent the inappropriate use of resource revenues. The chapter discusses the objectives of earmarking, to what extent it may help achieve them, and the costs it may entail.
- *The resource price or revenue in the budget* (chapter 10). Countries use a wide array of approaches to determine the reference resource price or resource revenue in the annual budget. Many resource-rich countries have tended to use conservative assumptions, motivated among other things by a desire to reduce fiscal risk or address spending pressures. The chapter provides a critical overview and discussion of country practices and offers some suggestions.

The significant diversity of resource-rich countries should be borne in mind in what follows. Many topics discussed in this volume will be more relevant to some resource-rich countries than to others. Country-specific factors that vary widely across resource-rich countries include the type of nonrenewable resources exploited, the level of development, the degree of capital scarcity, the stock of reserves in the ground, fiscal dependence on resource revenue, fiscal and financial positions, institutional capacity, the strength of PFM systems, intergovernmental relations, and fiscal transparency, governance, and accountability. Fiscal frame-works need to be adapted to the specific circumstances of each country.

Many issues and aspects of fiscal management discussed in the volume are illustrated with country examples. In some cases, selective lists of countries that implemented particular fiscal management mechanisms are provided. The examples do not necessarily imply that the policies, mechanisms, or procedures are still in place. Examples cited may refer to approaches that were in place in the past but that were subsequently changed.

PART I

The Challenges Posed by Resource Revenues

CHAPTER 1

What Complicates Fiscal Management in Resource-Rich Countries?

Resource revenue poses challenges to the formulation and implementation of fiscal policies and public financial management (PFM) in resource-rich countries.

First, resource revenue is volatile and uncertain. This is mainly because resource prices are highly volatile (figure 1.1). Perhaps even more important, resource prices are highly unpredictable, as shown by large ex-post projection errors (figure 1.2). Other sources of uncertainty include the size of resource reserves, future production volumes and costs, possible changes in future fiscal regimes, and the volatility of the real exchange rate. The uncertainty of resource revenue leads to uncertainty regarding government cash flow and government net wealth. This complicates budget planning, fiscal management, and the efficient use of public resources, particularly when resource revenue makes up a large share of total government revenue.

Figure 1.1 Developments in Global Oil and Copper Prices, 1970–2012

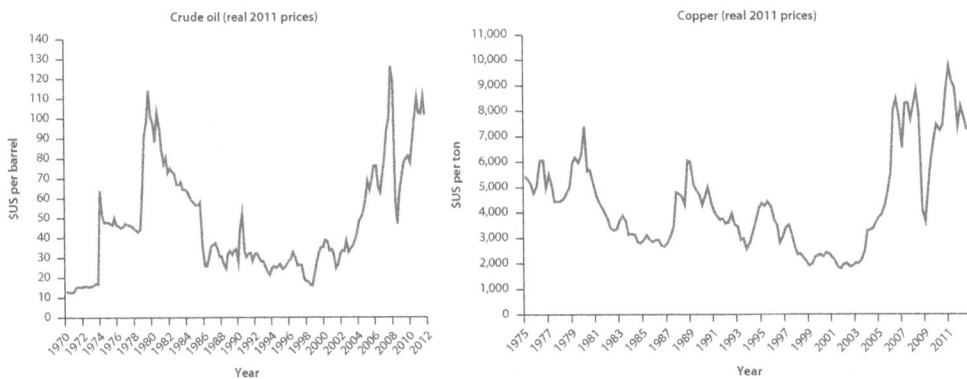

Source: IMF WEO database. Reprinted from IMF (2012c).

Figure 1.2 Oil Price Forecasts and Outturns, 1970–2012

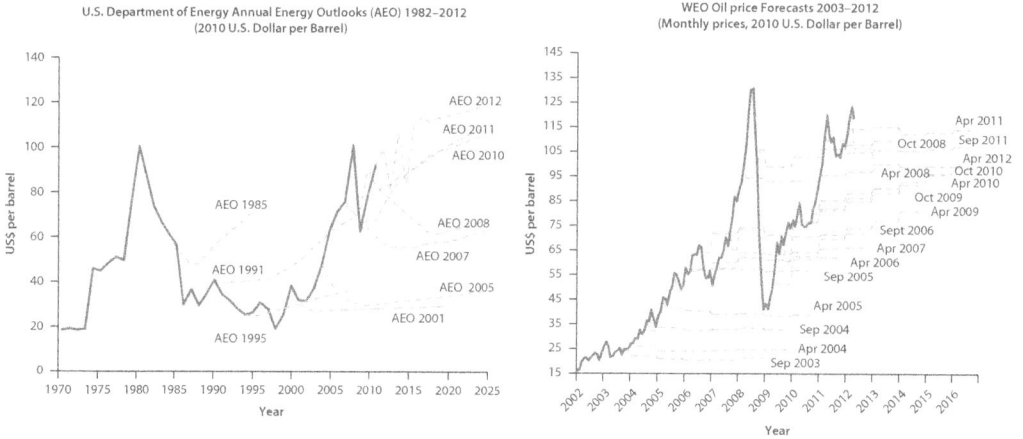

Sources: Reprinted from IMF (2012c).
Note: Solid lines on the left chart are spot West Texas Intermediate (WTI) oil prices; on the right chart are WEO averages of WTI and Fateh. The dashed lines are price projections.

For example, in the Republic of Congo, fiscal oil revenue fell by over half in real terms in 2009 from the previous year, as oil revenues declined from 40 percent of gross domestic product (GDP) in 2008 to 21 percent in 2009. In Angola the cash deficit of the central government increased by 3 percentage points of GDP in 2009—despite a reduction in government spending of over a third in real terms, prompted by financing concerns.[1]

Second, resource revenue arises from the exploitation of resources that are exhaustible and that run the risk of technological obsolescence. This raises complex questions regarding intergenerational equity, long-term fiscal sustainability, and asset allocation. According to BP, a number of oil producers heavily dependent on fiscal oil revenues (defined in this volume as countries where resource revenues are at least 20–25 percent of total fiscal revenues)—including Angola, the Republic of Congo, Equatorial Guinea, Mexico, Oman, and Trinidad and Tobago—have estimated proven oil reserves equivalent to only 10–20 years of production at current output levels (BP 2015).

Third, resource revenue largely originates from abroad. Hence, its fiscal use can have implications for the domestic economy, competitiveness, and macroeconomic stabilization. The effects of an external resource price boom in developing resource exporters are typically transmitted through fiscal policy, which can add to the appreciation of a nation's currency in real terms—and volatility—and thus hinder investment in the non-resource-traded sector.

Finally, the exploitation of nonrenewable resources can give rise to large rents, with associated political economy complications. In a number of resource-rich countries, resource revenue has been associated with poor-quality spending and rent seeking. Many oil producers that saw a rapid increase in public spending during the period of rising oil prices in the 2000s are characterized by low indices of government effectiveness and poor indicators of public investment efficiency, in part reflecting capacity constraints.

Revenues from oil and gas differ from mining revenues in some important and fiscally relevant respects:

- Oil rents (the excess of revenues over all costs of production as well as the "normal" rate of return on capital) are typically larger than mineral rents. Resource revenue as a share of total government revenue tends to be higher in oil-exporting countries (OECs) than in mining-exporting countries (MECs). In 2000–07 the average share of resource revenue in the total revenue of a representative sample of 37 OECs was 50 percent, compared with 11 percent in a sample of 10 MECs.[2]
- There are marked differences in standard fiscal regimes for oil and gas and for mining. For example, signature bonuses, production-sharing contracts, and state participation with paid equity are common in oil and gas, much less so in mining.
- The mining sector often comprises numerous companies of various sizes, exploiting various metals and minerals. The oil and gas sector is typically dominated by a smaller number of large companies extracting only those resources (Darby and Lempa 2007). On the other hand, joint ventures are more common in the oil sector, whereas individual mines tend to be operated by a single company.
- The participation of the state in the oil and gas sector is quite common, notably in the form of a national oil company. It is far less common in the mining sector. Fifteen of the largest oil companies in the world are state owned, whereas state mining companies are now rare.
- While oil and gas revenues are typically centralized and accrue to the central government (Canada and the United States being two notable exceptions), in the mining sector significant revenues often accrue to subnational (regional and local) levels of government.

On the other hand, the volatility of the annual average prices of oil and of key minerals has been similar. The standard deviations of the annual percentage change of the prices of oil, copper, iron ore, and tin in 1981–2015 were on the order of 25 percent.[3]

Notes

1. Authors' estimation from data in IMF (2012b) for the Republic of Congo, and the IMF's World Economic Outlook (WEO) database, April 2016, for Angola.
2. Calculation based on data in Daniel, Keen, and McPherson (2010).
3. Calculation based on the IMF's WEO annual average prices of these commodities.

PART II

Fiscal Policy, Stabilization, Sustainability, and Growth

CHAPTER 2

Fiscal Policy and Short-Run Stabilization

Fiscal policy in resource-rich countries has the same broad objectives as fiscal policy in other countries. It should contribute to the achievement of macroeconomic stability, sustainable and inclusive growth, and poverty reduction within a framework of fiscal sustainability.

Macroeconomic and Fiscal Stability

A recurrent challenge for resource-rich countries is how to manage the impact of volatile and uncertain resource revenues on macroeconomic and financial stability. Macroeconomic volatility in these countries often reflects—to a large extent, but not exclusively—resource revenue volatility and a high frequency of exogenous shocks in a context of significant export concentration. In resource-rich countries, volatility is one of the main ways in which any negative economic effects from the exploitation of natural resources are usually spread; according to van der Ploeg (2011), volatility may be the quintessence of the resource curse.

There are strong macroeconomic, public financial management (PFM), and risk management arguments for smoothing public spending at prudent and sustainable levels in the face of volatile and uncertain resource revenue streams in the short run.

Macroeconomic Rationale

Macroeconomic stability is important for high and sustainable rates of economic growth. And growth, in turn, is a key factor influencing poverty. Hence, macroeconomic stability is a key component of any poverty reduction strategy (IMF and World Bank 2001).

There is strong empirical evidence that macroeconomic volatility and uncertainty have adverse effects on long-term growth, poverty reduction, and income distribution. Such effects are exacerbated in low-income countries (LICs), in countries with limited financial development, and in developing countries that are unable to conduct countercyclical fiscal policies, that is, policies aimed at reducing the cyclical tendencies in the economy.[1]

What, then, are the main channels through which significant exogenous volatility can affect growth? Volatility and uncertainty have adverse effects on private investment: as they increase, so do the risks faced by investors, who may have to reallocate resources to accommodate sudden and large changes in demand and relative prices, and cope with the volatility of the real exchange rate (including episodes of "Dutch disease" during booms).[2] Thus, private investment is a key channel for the negative effect of volatility on growth (Aizenman and Marion 1999; Kose, Prasad, and Terrones 2005; Van der Ploeg and Poelhekke 2010).

Volatility can increase income inequality, and there is growing evidence that high income inequality is detrimental to long-term growth. Channels through which volatility affects income inequality include inflation (a regressive tax that hurts the poor in particular), volatile public social spending, and the fact that volatility increases the vulnerability of households with credit constraints. The impact of volatility on income inequality is more pronounced in LICs than in other countries.

Further, persistent instability often acts as a barrier to the diversification and deepening of financial systems. Macroeconomic stability is important for financial sector development. Higher levels of financial system development are associated with lower output volatility in resource-rich countries (as in other countries), with positive implications for growth—up to a point: financial sector deepening seems to have a U-shaped effect on macroeconomic volatility, with very high financial depth (as observed in many developed countries) amplifying consumption and investment volatility.

Exogenous shocks are only part of the story—fiscal policy can magnify the impact of these shocks. In resource-rich countries, fiscal policy, given its crucial role in injecting part of the revenue from resources into the domestic economy, is a particularly important tool for short-term macroeconomic management. Fiscal volatility, sudden changes in public spending, the nonresource balance (NRB, defined as the difference between nonresource revenues and nonresource expenditures),[3] and procyclicality in fiscal policy contribute to macroeconomic volatility and uncertainty.

In resource-rich countries, private sector investment and consumption are often procyclical with resource prices. When resource prices are good, the private sector is confident and increases its spending. Credit can become abundant, but if there are domestic supply constraints, the economy may overheat. There may be upward pressures on the exchange rate, and high spending levels can contribute to inflating asset bubbles. By raising public spending at the same time, which often happens in these circumstances, the government contributes to the overheating.

There is therefore a strong macroeconomic case for smoothing public expenditure and the NRB in the face of resource revenue fluctuations. Reducing policy-induced volatility contributes to reducing macroeconomic volatility and hence fostering growth and development.

In its work with resource-rich countries, the World Bank has often advised smoothing public expenditure. For example, in the Lao People's Democratic Republic (PDR) it advised the adoption of a fiscal policy that smoothes government spending over time, which would help manage the volatility of revenues while also helping save for times when revenues are low (World Bank 2010a). In Kazakhstan, the World Bank explored the role of fiscal policy over the business cycle in a context of volatile resource revenue, and estimated the welfare gains from adopting fiscal policies to smooth the volatility of private consumption (World Bank 2013a).

Public Financial Management Rationale

There are PFM arguments for stabilizing public expenditure. Large and sudden fluctuations in public spending can entail fiscal costs, including in the quality and efficiency of spending. The level of spending needs to be determined taking into account its likely quality and the capacity of government to execute it efficiently. The sudden creation or enlargement of spending programs—including public investment—in a context of rising resource prices or volumes can overwhelm the public administration's capacity to design, manage, and execute expenditure efficiently.

If the private sector is booming when resource prices are rising, the costs faced by the public sector may increase amid supply bottlenecks. In particular, large public investment programs can overwhelm capacity in the construction sector and put upward pressure on the prices of construction services as well as other nontradable goods.

Conversely, sudden fiscal adjustments, prompted by falls in resource prices, and lack of access to financing have often led to abrupt and inefficient cuts in public expenditure, frequently concentrated on investment. For example, as oil prices fell precipitously starting in mid-2008, government investment in the Islamic Republic of Iran in fiscal year (FY) 2009/10 was reduced by more than a quarter in real terms relative to the previous fiscal year.[4]

Fiscal Risk Management Rationale

Large fiscal expansions during boom times can increase fiscal risks and vulnerabilities. If resource prices fall following a boom, the associated resource revenue declines may, depending on the availability of financing, require rapid and painful fiscal and exchange rate adjustments, with costs in terms of procyclicality, inefficiency, and impact on social expenditures. At the same time, many expenditure programs are difficult to contain or streamline following expansions, with potential negative implications for fiscal sustainability. This is discussed further in chapter 3.

Cyclicality of Fiscal Policy in Resource-Rich Countries

Fiscal policy has generally been found to be procyclical in developing countries (Talvi and Végh 2005; Kraay and Servén 2013). Procyclicality has been particularly prevalent in resource-rich countries, with implications for macroeconomic and fiscal volatility and uncertainty (Frankel 2011).[5]

Where fiscal policies have been procyclical, they have contributed to macroeconomic instability, volatility, and damaging boom-and-bust episodes.[6] They have also put pressure on PFM systems, reduced the quality of spending (including in the execution of public investment plans), and increased long-term uncertainties.

For example, government expenditures in many oil-exporting emerging markets and developing economies have closely followed oil prices in recent commodity price cycles (figure 2.1):

• As oil prices rose from 2003, the median annual rate of increase of expenditure in real terms surged to 15 percent in 2005–08. For African oil exporters, the median annual rate of increase was 20 percent a year.
• Then oil prices fell from mid-2008, and in 2009 the price decline year on year was 36 percent—an annual price change not unusual in the oil market.[7] Expenditures were reduced on average in 2009. Many oil exporters that had increased spending very fast during the upswing were forced to procyclically

Figure 2.1 Emerging Market and Developing Economy Oil Exporters: Median Annual Percentage Change of General Government Expenditure in Real Terms and Oil Prices, 2004–15

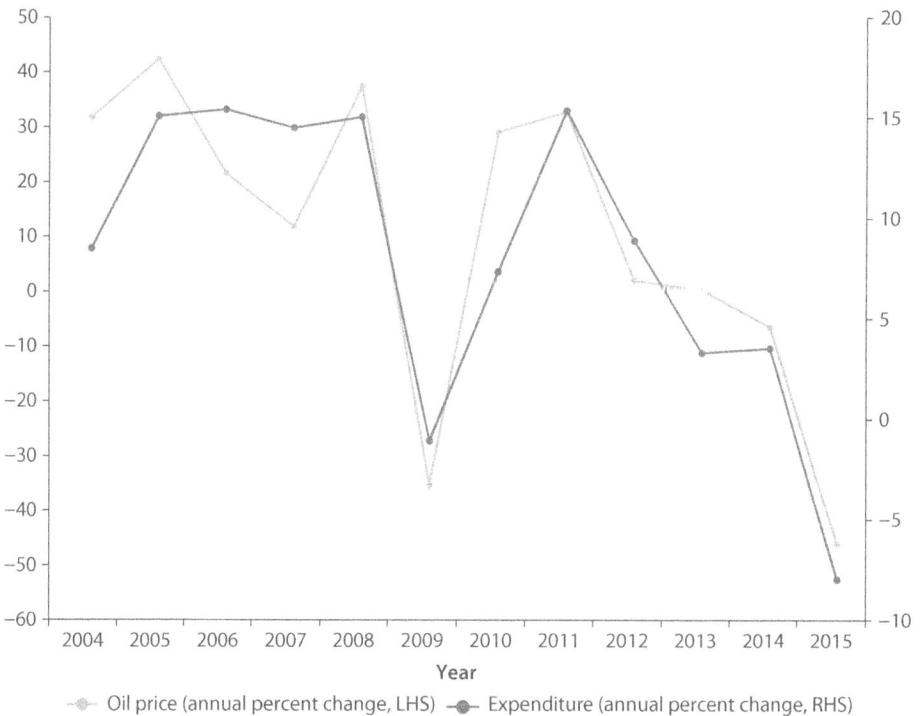

Source: Calculations based on data from the IMF's WEO (April 2016).
Note: Government expenditure deflated by the consumer price index (CPI). Oil-exporting countries included in the sample are: Algeria, Angola, Azerbaijan, Bahrain, Bolivia, Brunei Darussalam, Cameroon, Chad, Colombia, the Democratic Republic of Congo, Ecuador, Equatorial Guinea, Gabon, Islamic Republic of Iran, Kazakhstan, Kuwait, Libya, Nigeria, Oman, Qatar, the Russian Federation, Saudi Arabia, Timor-Leste, Trinidad and Tobago, Turkmenistan, the United Arab Emirates, República Bolivariana de Venezuela, and Republic of Yemen.

cut expenditure and contract their non-oil deficits, at least in part, because of their precarious financial positions, insufficient savings, and lack of financing—though concerns about the possible protracted nature of the price decline may have played a role as well.

- As oil prices recovered in 2010–12, spending resumed its strong upward trend.
- Expenditures continued to rise at a slower pace in 2013–14 as oil prices remained elevated through mid-2014.
- The substantial fall in the price of oil in the second half of 2014 and in 2015— by close to 50 percent year on year—prompted severe cuts in expenditure among many oil producers. In 2015, the median expenditure cut was over 8 percent in real terms—but it was 15 percent among African oil producers. Expenditure in real terms was reduced in more than four-fifths of the countries in the sample; in six of these countries, expenditure was cut by more than a quarter. Further expenditure reductions were projected in many countries for 2016. The few countries that did not reduce expenditure in real terms in 2015 tended to be countries that had comparatively moderate spending increases in 2004–14.

Consistent with figure 2.1, the IMF (2015a) finds that government spending growth has been positively correlated with commodity prices. This procyclical response has exacerbated rather than mitigated the effect of resource price volatility on the economy, and may have hampered economic growth. Adding to this procyclicality, governments have tended to loosen their fiscal stance when the domestic nonresource economy strengthened, and to tighten it when the economy weakened.

Similarly, Villafuerte and López-Murphy (2010) find that the fiscal policies of oil-exporting countries (OECs) were generally procyclical during the boom period 2003–08, and that they remained procyclical, on average, during the 2009 oil price downturn. Furthermore, evidence from Latin America suggests that countries displaying more conservative fiscal policies during the boom were able to implement more expansionary (countercyclical) fiscal policies, on average, during the 2009 crisis (Villafuerte, López-Murphy, and Ossowski 2010). And the countries that had had the most procyclical fiscal responses during the boom were, by 2009–10, the most vulnerable to resource price shocks.[8]

The procyclicality of credit markets should also be taken into account. Easy credit conditions during upswings may provide incentives for procyclical borrowing. During downturns, credit availability is often reduced when external financing may be most needed.

For a countercyclical policy to be effective and credible, and in some cases even feasible, public net debt needs to be low. Countries with high debt levels are often unable to accommodate resource revenue downturns due to financing constraints related to liquidity, sustainability, and other policy concerns—or a countercyclical fiscal policy response would generate sovereign risk concerns.

These countries are likely to be best served by placing a high priority on reducing debt and sovereign risk premiums, to enable the adoption of countercyclical fiscal policies during downturns.

Therefore, countries with weak financial positions would do well to pursue fiscal strategies to set the conditions for breaking the procyclical response of spending to volatile resource prices. Strategies to moderate expansionary fiscal policy biases during resource booms—and reduce the nonresource deficit over time—would create fiscal room that might be needed when a transitory resource boom ends.

A strong fiscal position is also essential to allow for an orderly adjustment to catastrophic resource shocks that turn out to be long lasting. A long-lasting decline in resource prices, such as the oil market collapse of 1986, may prompt major solvency reassessments and thus require adjustment to restore sustainability. A country with a strong financial position can afford to adjust the nonresource deficit in a gradual and orderly fashion.

The political economy of government spending in resource-rich countries often conspires against making fiscal policy less procyclical. A substantial body of literature has analyzed this issue. For example, Tornell and Lane (1999) postulate the existence of a "voracity effect" in countries with weak legal and political institutions and multiple powerful groups that interact dynamically via the fiscal process. Positive revenue shocks then generate more than proportional increases in government expenditure relative to the windfalls, as the budget process succumbs to pressures.

Efforts to strengthen fiscal transparency and accountability can help mitigate the political economy problems often associated with managing resource rents. They could include, as needed, disclosing analyses of fiscal risk, setting up medium-term expenditure frameworks (MTEFs), building constituencies in favor of prudent fiscal policies (including through public information and education programs), extending the time horizon of public debates, and strengthening institutions in general. Barma and others (2012) provide a detailed discussion of governance and political economy issues in resource-rich countries. See also Eifert, Gelb, and Tallroth (2003) and Sinnott, Nash, and de la Torre (2010) in a Latin American context.

The assessment of the cyclicality of fiscal policy in resource-rich countries is more challenging than in other countries and raises a number of methodological issues. Appendix B discusses the main approaches that have been used to estimate cyclically adjusted fiscal positions in resource-rich countries.

Coordination with Monetary Policy and the Dilemmas of Sterilization

The short-run management of volatile resource revenue can pose challenges to the coordination of monetary and fiscal policies. Fiscal policies in particular play a crucial role:

- If the government saves a resource windfall abroad, for example, in a sovereign wealth fund (SWF), or it spends it on imports, there are no domestic monetary implications, and currency appreciation is likely to be limited.

- If the government saves the windfall domestically, placing deposits with domestic banks or repaying domestic debt, this will increase domestic liquidity. The move could well be expansionary and inflationary; this will depend on what the banks and others do with the additional resources, and on the degree of capital mobility.
- If the government repays domestic debt, and the central bank sterilizes the liquidity injection, one form of public debt (on the government's balance sheet) is exchanged for another (on the central bank's balance sheet).[9] Government interest costs will go down, but a rise in central bank interest costs will be reflected in lower profit transfers from the central bank to the government. The central bank could also raise reserve requirements to reduce liquidity, but this policy would be effective only to the extent that there are no excess bank reserves.

Often, governments want to spend windfalls but do not want to face the inflation and real appreciation consequences—and they also want to retain international reserves. So the central bank is called upon to sterilize the liquidity injections arising from the higher nonresource deficit, financed with higher resource revenue and other foreign exchange inflows.

Sterilization will tend to raise interest rates and crowd out private investment. The domestic banks, instead of lending to the private sector, lend to the central bank. In effect, there is a switch from private investment to government consumption or investment. Sterilization is also likely to be difficult and costly in resource-rich countries with thin domestic financial markets. The costs of sterilization can be significant when a lot of liquidity is sterilized and interest rate differentials are large. Sterilization can generate central bank losses that may have to be financed with yet more base money creation, in an escalating spiral. Moreover, sterilization may be self-defeating to the extent that the higher interest rates also attract foreign capital inflows.

The ministry of finance (MoF) and the central bank may disagree over who should bear the burden of the required short-run stabilization policies and the preservation of competitiveness. The central bank will often want the MoF to reduce government spending to relieve the pressure on monetary policy. The ministry will often want to maintain spending and have the central bank sterilize the liquidity injections, something that the bank may find politically difficult if it has to explain the resulting losses to parliament and the public.

In sum, fiscal/monetary policy coordination issues and the development of financial systems argue for prudent fiscal policies during windfalls. A smooth and gradual fiscal response to a windfall can limit the impact on inflation and the real exchange rate, and facilitate the task of the central bank.

Resource Revenues and Fiscal Federalism

In resource-rich countries with federal structures, fiscal federalism and intergovernmental relations are an important political, structural, macroeconomic, and fiscal issue. The assignment of revenues and expenditure responsibilities to various levels of government, as well as intergovernmental relations and coordination, raise a number of extremely complex issues. These include:

- The assignment of tax bases, and whether subnational regions should have the right to raise resource revenues;
- The assignment of expenditure responsibilities;
- The ability of subnational governments (SNGs) to cope with resource revenue volatility given their expenditure assignments;
- PFM and the challenges it poses to SNGs that may have limited administrative and institutional capacity;
- The design of intergovernmental transfers to achieve some desired degree of vertical and horizontal balance and equity without endangering macroeconomic stability;
- The control of subnational borrowing, particularly given moral hazard problems;
- The coordination of fiscal policy between the federal government and the SNGs, to help bring about desired macroeconomic objectives;
- The capacity of regional and local government authorities to undertake the highly technical task of administering tax and royalty regimes for the extractive industries (EI) sector, if those revenues are assigned to them; and
- Environmental and social concerns.

A discussion of these issues lies outside the scope of this volume. Interested readers are referred to Ter-Minassian (1997) and Ahmad and Brosio (2006, 2015) for broad discussions of fiscal federalism issues. Fiscal federalism issues in the specific resource-rich country context are discussed in Anderson (2012), who covers the features of oil and gas revenue management in 12 federal resource-rich countries; Ahmad and Mottu (2003) and Brosio (2003).

Notes

1. Hnatkovska and Loayza (2005) find that macroeconomic volatility and long-run growth are negatively related, and that this negative link is exacerbated in countries unable to conduct countercyclical fiscal policies (see below). See also Pinto (1987), Ramey and Ramey (1995), Auty and Mikesell (1998), Auty (2001), Gelb (2002), Devlin and Lewin (2005), and Loayza and others (2007).

2. "Dutch disease" refers to the tendency for large resource revenues to appreciate the currency in real terms, which then damages the nonresource tradable sector. Foreign revenue inflows that are spent (by the government and/or the private sector) lead to an increase in domestic demand relative to domestic supply, which can increase the prices of nontradable goods and services, and cause an appreciation of the currency in real terms. See Fatás and Mihov (2003, 2005), Aizenman and Pinto (2005), and Aghion and Banerjee (2005).

3. The nonresource balance (NRB) abstracts from revenue fluctuations arising from changes in international resource prices, from changes in resource production volumes

and costs, and from other resource-related factors. See appendix A for a detailed discussion of fiscal indicators for the analysis of fiscal policy in resource-rich countries.

4. Authors' estimation from data in the International Monetary Fund (IMF 2011a), using the consumer price index (CPI) as deflator.

5. For example, based on the IMF's World Economic Outlook (WEO) data, the volatility of central government spending (measured as the standard deviation of annual percentage changes of expenditure in real terms, deflated by the CPI) among Sub-Saharan African oil-exporting countries (OECs) in 2001–13 was about one-third higher than that of Sub-Saharan African oil importers. In some countries, the volatility of government expenditure has been very high, with standard deviations in excess of 15 percent.

6. Gelb and Garsmann (2010) argue that the loss from underspending during booms is modest, whereas the loss from overspending is potentially very large.

7. In 2009 the average international oil price in U.S. dollars, as measured in the IMF's WEO average of oil prices, fell by 36 percent compared with 2008. Since 1973 the annual change in the oil price has been greater than 30 percent, on average, in close to one year out of every three.

8. See also Husain, Tazhibayeva, and Ter-Martirosyan (2008), Sturm, Gurtner, and González Alegre (2009), and Frankel (2011).

9. Central banks often resort to sterilization to reduce the threat of inflation and/or currency appreciation. Sterilization typically involves the use of open market operations. For example, the central bank sells its own paper or treasury bills to absorb liquidity.

CHAPTER 3

Managing Fiscal Risks and Vulnerabilities

Fiscal Risks

Risk refers to uncertainty about future events and outcomes. In a risk management context, when actions and future states of nature have more than one possible outcome, risk refers to the effect of uncertainty on objectives.

In public finance, fiscal risk has been defined as the possibility of short- to medium-term deviations in fiscal variables (such as revenues, expenditures, fiscal balances, assets and liabilities, and off-balance-sheet items such as guarantees) from what was expected at the time of the budget or other forecast (Cebotari and others 2009; Allen and Vani 2013; Petrie 2013). Government and business plans often focus on a particular outcome (the plan, or central scenario), and other possible outcomes are "deviations" from that scenario.

Fiscal risks can be broken down into *general economic risks* and *specific risks*, and also into *explicit risks* and *implicit risks* (Petrie 2013).

General economic risks arise from the volatility of macroeconomic variables— such as the rate of growth, inflation, the exchange rate, interest rates, and (notably in resource-rich countries) resource revenues—and other large exogenous events. For example, the rate of growth may affect fiscal revenues and expenditures; the public debt may be affected by the depreciation of the currency or by increases in interest rates. *Specific risks* are narrower and have a bearing on public finances through more specific channels. For example, debt guarantees may require the government to pay if specific events occur.

Explicit risks involve the existence of explicit, contingent government obligations or liabilities whose realization, timing, and magnitude depend on uncertain future events beyond the control of the government. *Implicit risks* are present in situations where, although there is no explicit commitment or obligation on the government to provide support should a specific event occur, there is an expectation that the government would step in for a variety of political, economic, or other reasons.

Resource Revenue Dependence and General Fiscal Risks

Fiscal policy in resource-rich countries must take into account the enormous volatility and uncertainty of resource revenue—this is one of the key fiscal risks affecting public finances in countries dependent on resource revenues. Yet in many resource-rich countries, the short-term horizons of annual budgets do not give adequate weight to resource revenue risks in the medium term and some-times even in the short term. This contributes to the procyclical expenditure patterns described in chapter 2, which in turn exacerbate fiscal vulnerabilities to downturns. Fiscal vulnerability is concerned with the extent to which a country is exposed to the risk of a fiscal crisis (Hemming 2013a).

During booms, spending often adjusts to available current revenue without a full understanding of the risks generated. In particular, some expenditure pro-grams, once created or increased, are difficult to reverse (hysteresis). This includes entitlement programs, wages and public sector employment, and multi-year capital projects that give rise to future recurrent expenditures.

As spending is increased, the probability of large and costly fiscal adjustments later may rise as well. This is because the nonresource fiscal position becomes more exposed to shocks as a result of the increase in spending *during the boom*—and the *future* increases in spending needed to operate the new investments. Annual budgets that ignore risk and uncertainty going forward, and that are not linked to medium- and long-term policies and plans, can create additional spend-ing hysteresis and new multiyear spending commitments that entrench rigidities, exacerbate fiscal risks, and ultimately undermine fiscal discipline.

As a practical matter, in a number of resource-rich countries fiscal vulnerabil-ity to resource shocks increased during the resource price boom, despite the surge in resource prices (York and Zhan 2009; Villafuerte, López-Murphy, and Ossowski 2010). This was mainly due to large expenditure increases. Additional factors that may have played a role, depending on the country, include the appre-ciation of the currency in real terms, which reduced the domestic purchasing power of resource revenue, and a low elasticity of nonresource revenue to non-resource gross domestic product (NRGDP), which would contribute to the deterioration of nonresource balances (NRBs).

Between 2004 and 2014, the fiscal positions of many countries became more exposed to oil price downturns. Specifically, the median general government fis-cal balance of oil-exporting emerging markets and developing economies deteriorated by 7 percentage points of gross domestic product (GDP) in 2014 compared to 2004 (figure 3.1). This happened in spite of a 155 percent nominal increase in oil prices over the same period. And although the average nominal oil price in 2015 was similar to the price 10 years earlier, the median fiscal deficit was worse by 11 percentage points of GDP, fiscal adjustment measures in a number of countries notwithstanding.

In 2014 two-thirds of the oil-exporting countries (OECs) in the sample (and almost all African oil exporters) were running general government deficits despite elevated oil prices. While the net public debt of many oil exporters

Figure 3.1 Emerging Market and Developing Economy Oil Exporters: Median General Government Balances and Oil Prices, 2004–15

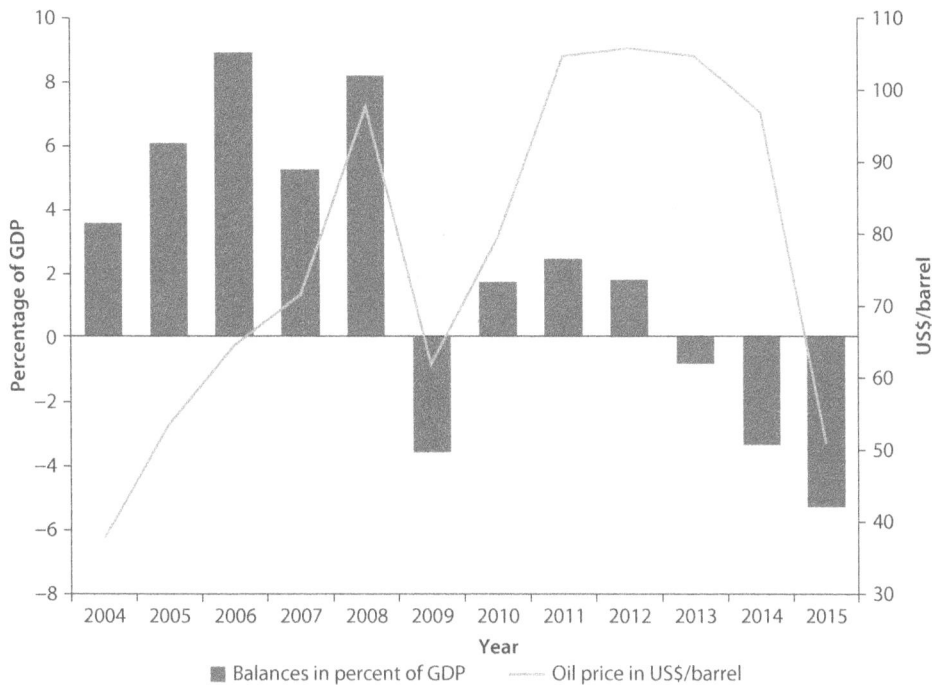

Source: Calculations based on data from the IMF's WEO (April 2016).
Note: Median general government balances as a share of GDP. Oil prices are the simple average of spot prices of Dated Brent, West Texas Intermediate (WTI), and Dubai Fateh, as reported in the IMF's WEO. Oil-exporting countries (OECs) as in figure 2.1. GDP = gross domestic product.

declined after 2004—as surpluses allowed for the repayment of debt and/or the buildup of financial assets—the fiscal positions of a number of countries were vulnerable to even moderate oil price shocks, mainly as a result of weaker NRBs.

Between 2008 and 2013 the median fiscal breakeven oil price (at which the fiscal accounts are in balance at current levels of the non-oil balance and oil output) of Middle East and North Africa (MENA) oil exporters almost doubled to about $100/barrel (barrel of oil—bbl) (IMF 2008, 2013a) (figure 3.2).[1] Some of these countries significantly increased public sector wages and entitlements (expenditure components that, once ratcheted up, may be difficult to reduce).

By 2015 most oil exporters in the MENA region could not balance their budgets at an oil price of $60/bbl (IMF 2015b). Given the decline in the average annual oil price, the median general government overall fiscal balance deteriorated in 2015 by 11 percentage points of GDP from the previous year, to a median deficit of 15 percent of GDP despite fiscal adjustment measures in several countries. Estimated fiscal breakeven oil prices rose substantially in other countries as well (Deutsche Bank 2014). Following the decline in oil prices in 2014–15, oil prices in early 2016 were well below the estimated fiscal breakeven oil prices in a large number of OECs.

Figure 3.2 Fiscal Breakeven Oil Prices of Middle East and North Africa Oil Exporters, 2008 and 2013

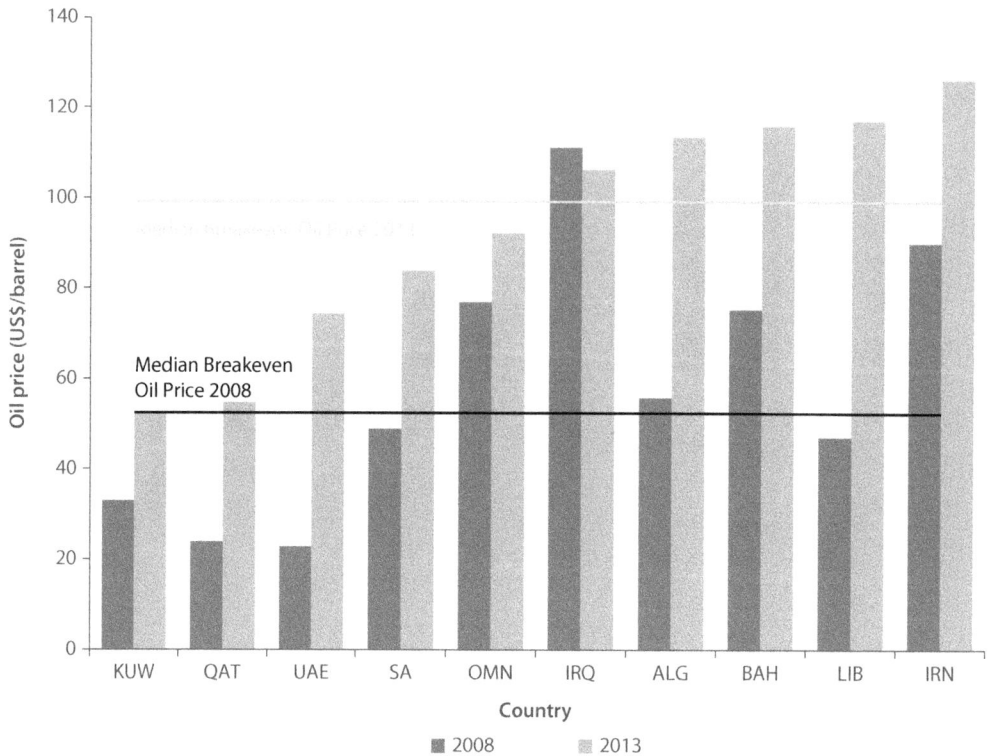

Source: IMF (2008, 2013a).
Note: The fiscal breakeven oil price is the price at which the fiscal accounts are in balance at current levels of the non-oil balance and oil output.

Against this background, a sound assessment of the risks posed by resource revenues and the establishment of risk management strategies could help the framing of fiscal policies in a number of resource-rich countries. For this purpose, it is necessary to use risk analysis to evaluate proposed spending paths in the medium term—how resilient are they to shocks? Scenario or stress tests examining the impact of potential negative resource and other shocks on the budget balance and financing needs to be regularly conducted, particularly in light of asymmetric costs of adjustment.

Liquidity buffers can protect spending in the event of adverse resource revenue shocks. Their optimal size will depend on the degree of resource dependence, policy objectives, and risk tolerance (box 3.1).

Exogenous general fiscal risks can sometimes be mitigated through the use of financial instruments. In the case of resource-exporting countries, resource price risks could be hedged by the government (to hedge resource-related budget revenue) or by the national resource companies (if relevant). Hedging transfers risk to financial markets that may be better able to bear it, at a cost (IMF and World Bank 2011).

Box 3.1 Fiscal Risk Analysis in Resource-Rich Countries

Probabilistic analyses, using historical parameters of the stochastic process driving resource prices, can be used to determine the optimal size of financial assets to stabilize spending in the face of shocks.

Value-at-risk (VaR) analysis is an example of this approach. It can be used by resource-rich countries to assess the optimal size of a liquidity pool, given the stochastic process driving resource revenue. The resulting buffer would be used to absorb resource revenue volatility (IMF 2012a, 2015a). How much liquidity is needed to ensure, with a given degree of confidence, that the buffer is unlikely to be depleted over a specific time horizon, given a fiscal policy as embodied in the nonresource balance (NRB)?

Price shocks can be modeled in various ways: for example, by deducting from the projected prices for the next n years the standard deviation of 1- to n-year changes in real oil prices (estimated from historical data); or by applying the distribution of the relevant forecast errors around each resource futures price on the basis of historical forecast errors of future prices with respect to actual spot prices at various future time horizons. Fan charts that show a forecasted baseline and ranges for possible deviations—with their estimated probabilities—can then be used.

The VaR results would be used to help calibrate country-specific target levels for the NRB, contingency reserves, and liquidity cushions from a fiscal vulnerability perspective.

A simulation for Nigeria, for example, suggests that the country would need to have a precautionary buffer stock of about 60 percent of annual oil revenue to be reasonably confident that a smooth government spending path can be maintained over three years (Baunsgaard and others 2012; see also Bartsch 2006).

Simulations for Gabon made a few years ago indicated that a minimum buffer of Communauté Financière Africaine Franc (CFAF) 750 billion, equivalent to about 30 percent of annual oil revenue in 2012, would be needed to ensure, with a probability of 85 percent, that the buffer is not fully depleted over a three-year period (IMF 2013b).

Model-based approaches also seek to determine the likelihood that a NRB path can be maintained given resource revenue volatility. They are more complex and require more information than VaR approaches, because they link fiscal policy to the macroeconomy, and take macro feedbacks into account. (See IMF [2012a] for operational details regarding the practical implementation of the VaR and model-based approaches.)

For example, model-based simulations for Angola compared a gradual approach to the buildup of public investment to a more aggressive one. They suggested that a fiscal scenario involving the rapid scaling up of public investment would be consistent with building a liquidity buffer, but with a 30 percent probability that the buffer would be insufficient to prevent future expenditure reductions. The model also revealed that an aggressive approach would be associated with a worse outcome for non-oil gross domestic product (GDP) because the inability to protect spending from shocks would result in volatile investment rates (IMF 2012a).

Source: Authors, based on sources noted in box.

For example, the budget in Mexico is vulnerable to oil price uncertainty and volatility, as taxes and levies paid by Petróleos Mexicanos (PEMEX) (the national oil company) typically contribute over one-third of federal revenue. The ministry of finance (MoF) has implemented since the 1990s a hedging program based on put options that sets a minimum oil strike price to be received. This approach, underpinned by strong institutional arrangements, limits downward oil price risks (Yépez-García and Dana 2012). The mechanism has helped moderate the effects of oil price volatility on the federal budget; it is discussed in detail in IMF and World Bank (2011).

The use of market instruments to reduce risk requires considerable technical capacity and strong governance, and is best not attempted if those elements are not in place. Risk management programs involving the use of derivatives require deep understanding of risk, volatility, and financial instruments; expertise; and a strong institutional framework to ensure internal risk control procedures, monitoring, reporting, and evaluation. These mechanisms are needed to limit the risk of strategic and execution errors and to forestall speculation. Yépez-García and Dana (2012) discuss the institutional prerequisites that need to be in place before the use of hedging instruments can be considered.

Prudent Fiscal Policies as a Pro-Poor Strategy

A clarification of the trade-offs between spending and precautionary savings is in order. In developing resource-rich countries widespread poverty and urgent developmental needs would naturally suggest that—consistent with macroeconomic stability, and if there is appropriate capacity to implement productive spending programs, including investment—fiscal resources may be spent, rather than financial assets accumulated. It may be appropriate to increase public consumption if this contributes to reducing poverty and inequality, and increase investment to accelerate economic development. It may seem paradoxical for lower-income resource-rich countries to finance richer countries by accumulating foreign assets.

What is perhaps less widely recognized is that, given that these countries' access to credit is often procyclical, having precautionary financial assets is also a strong pro-poor and developmental strategy. It facilitates the implementation of countercyclical fiscal policy when needed. Reducing the volatility of household incomes, and raising the income of the most vulnerable during recessions and downturns, is a pro-poor strategy. But in order to be able to accomplish this, governments need to have precautionary financial assets at their disposal (Engel, Neilsen, and Valdés 2010; Laursen and Mahajan 2005). Recent empirical analysis by the World Bank confirms the importance of saving in good times to protect low-income groups during downturns.[2]

Botswana, Chile, and Peru are examples of resource-rich countries that were able to undertake countercyclical fiscal policies in the downturn of 2009, because of the solid fiscal positions they had built over the previous years. These countries used accumulated fiscal savings to finance significant fiscal stimulus packages that helped support activity, sustain employment, mitigate the impact on vulnerable social groups, and avoid a credit crunch.

For example, Botswana was able to accommodate a swing of 17 percentage points of GDP in the central government's overall balance, from a surplus of 5 percent of GDP in fiscal year 2007/08 to a deficit of 12 percent of GDP in 2009/10. This sharp deterioration reflected the fiscal impact of the collapse in the demand for diamonds during the global financial crisis and, more important, a substantial countercyclical easing of fiscal policy (including measures such as a public works program) to cushion the impact of difficulties in the diamond sector on the rest of the economy. This contributed to a healthy growth of non-mining GDP of close to 5 percent in 2009 despite the crisis (IMF 2011b, 2012d).

Resource Dependence and Specific Fiscal Risks

New or prospective petroleum or mineral producers that have been financially constrained may suddenly have access to a much larger resource envelope to meet their development needs. Large resources may also facilitate access to international capital markets and the financing of investment through instruments such as private-public partnerships (PPPs)—where the private sector supplies assets and services traditionally provided by the government—and the granting of guarantees to state-owned enterprises (SOEs), the private sector, or the banking system, backed by a stronger fiscal position.

However, government guarantees and PPPs can easily bypass expenditure controls, move costly public investment off-budget, shift debt off the government balance sheet, and hide the high cost of contractual arrangements that may have had to be granted to obtain private financing. Thus, fiscal risks rise because of the accumulation of contingent liabilities. In Colombia, for example, in early PPPs in the 1990s demand risk was retained by the government, in the form of significant guarantees to road concessionaires. Many of these guarantees were triggered by a recession, with a fiscal cost of 2 percent of GDP (Cebotari 2008). Colombia has improved significantly its design of PPPs since, and more broadly is now one of Latin America's leaders in managing and disclosing fiscal risks.

There are a number of effective mechanisms to manage specific fiscal risks. In the case of PPPs, projects need to be considered and prioritized in the context of the government's overall investment strategy, the distribution of risks between the government and the private sector has to be carefully considered (some risks are better managed by contractors, others by the government), the government should not take on excessive risks, and there needs to be a strong legal framework for the PPP process.

More broadly, the management of specific risks involves their effective identification, which in turn requires public entities to assess and report fiscal risks to the MoF, and comprehensive disclosure of fiscal risks in budget documents. For example, Nigeria's Fiscal Responsibility Act requires that the annual budget be accompanied by a Fiscal Risk Appendix evaluating the fiscal and other related risks to the annual budget and specifying measures to be taken to offset the occurrence of such risks. Regulations limiting aggregate government exposure to guarantees and PPP-related risks can be helpful. It is important for the MoF to have the power to veto projects that entail excessive fiscal risks.

Notes

1. Excluding the Republic of Yemen. The data should be treated with caution, as certain expenditures in some countries could be bulky and one-off—for example, large capital projects.

2. Simulations made by the World Bank's Global Practice for Macroeconomic and Fiscal Management in 2015 suggested that if oil prices in 2015 were to be a third below their average level in 2014, the impact among oil exporters would be highly variable, since these exporters were not equally prepared to cope with the fall in oil prices. Not all of them used effectively the "good times" of $100-plus/bbl (barrel of oil). The effect of cheaper oil on any one resource-rich country depended on whether it created the external and fiscal buffers to cushion a fall in oil prices. And these macroeconomic buffers help protect the poor. Without buffers, an abrupt loss of resource export earnings means slower or negative growth, higher inflation, and less government revenue—that is, potentially lower employment, higher prices, and less social assistance, resulting in more poverty (Giugale 2015).

CHAPTER 4

Promoting Sustainability

Since nonrenewable resources are exhaustible and run the risk of obsolescence, countries have to consider how to allocate finite resource wealth to the current generation and to future generations. This has important implications for the decision of how much to consume and to save during the period of resource production, and how to allocate savings to different forms of assets. Furthermore, in some countries the need for fiscal saving also arises from long-term pressures on public finances, such as those of aging populations and growing health-care costs.

Fiscal frameworks require adaptation to the specific circumstances of each country. While macroeconomic stability would be a primary objective for all resource-rich countries, the priorities assigned to other objectives depend on specific country circumstances. In particular, key parameters to consider are fiscal resource dependence, that is, whether resource revenue is a large component of total fiscal revenue (indicative thresholds frequently used to denote significant fiscal dependence are on the order of 20–25 percent of total government revenue); whether resource revenue is seen as long lasting (with indicative thresholds for the reserve horizon—at current production rates—of at least 30–35 years) or temporary; whether the economy is capital scarce; and whether the absorptive and institutional capacities are limited or large.[1] Baunsgaard and others (2012) discuss priorities for fiscal frameworks depending on the country characteristics just indicated; they also provide a typology of developing resource-rich countries based on reserve horizons, and link it to different fiscal indicators and fiscal objectives.

For example, the fiscal frameworks of capital-scarce developing resource-rich countries with long production horizons would typically place emphasis on macroeconomic stability and developmental priorities, and would balance net financial asset accumulation with domestic public investment to foster growth (with improvements in public investment processes as needed). Long revenue horizons make sustainability concerns less pressing. In contrast, capital-rich developed resource-rich countries with short resource horizons would emphasize marcoeconomic stability and the accumulation of net financial savings to prepare for the period when the reserves run out.

Fiscal Sustainability Analysis in Resource-Rich Countries

Analyses of fiscal sustainability in developed and emerging countries are usually based on medium-term projections of the ratio of public debt to gross domestic product (GDP), given certain macroeconomic projections and fiscal policy assumptions. A typical debt-sustainability analysis (DSA) involves examining the expected trajectory of the debt ratio in the medium term, to assess whether the underlying fiscal policies can be sustained under plausible macroeconomic conditions without jeopardizing public sector solvency. In a growing number of countries, the time horizon for DSAs is being extended to account for long-term issues such as aging populations.

The International Monetary Fund (IMF) and the World Bank have recommended a specific debt sustainability framework for low-income countries (LICs). The standardized framework for analyzing debt-related vulnerabilities consists of a set of indicative policy-dependent thresholds against which projections of external public debt are compared to assess the risk of debt distress. Vulnerability to external and policy shocks is explored in alternative scenarios and standardized bound tests (IMF and World Bank 2012).

In resource-rich countries, particularly those with limited reserves, the sustainability analysis needs to include the exhaustibility of nonrenewable resources. The public balance sheet approach to fiscal statistics and fiscal analysis incorporates this element. Under this approach, the public sector's net worth is defined as the total stock of public sector financial and nonfinancial assets minus liabilities. Nonfinancial assets include petroleum and mineral reserves in the ground that are currently exploitable with existing technology and relative prices.[2] Changes in public sector net worth are an indicator of the sustainability of fiscal policies.

In addition, the projection period needs to be extended into the long term because nonrenewable resources give rise to important intergenerational allocation issues that make advisable the use of long-term intertemporal models. These exercises force the choice of explicit intertemporal welfare criteria regarding how much resource revenue to consume now, versus how much to save for future generations, and in what form.[3]

A number of fiscal sustainability exercises for resource-rich countries have been based on the permanent income hypothesis (PIH). These models provide a benchmark for the nonresource primary balance (NRPB) that can be financed indefinitely. The benchmark is defined as the permanent annual NRPB derived from estimated government net wealth—the expected present value of projected future fiscal oil revenues plus the value of net government financial assets.[4]

Long-term PIH fiscal sustainability models—in which no distinction is made between the consumption and investment components of the NRPB—have been challenged. It has been noted that the fiscal benchmarks these models prescribe are too tight for low-income resource-rich countries because they ignore the longer-term developmental needs in capital-scarce, credit-constrained countries and the potential role of productive public investment in that context (Van der Ploeg and Venables 2008; Collier and others 2009; Van der Ploeg 2011, 2012). In particular, if the economy is capital scarce, the rate of return to domestic capital is likely to be high, and may well be above world interest rates.[5] Thus, it is important how policy makers allocate public savings during the production period, into net accumulation of foreign financial assets, and investment in domestic physical and human capital, to promote growth.

In low-income resource-rich countries, investing resource revenues domestically could relieve existing large deficits in infrastructure and human capital. Investment could relieve capital scarcity, raise potential nonresource growth, and increase fiscal revenues. In these circumstances, the optimal NRPB will be lower than the benchmark NRPB suggested by PIH models, as productive public investment is scaled up—provided the government can realize the fiscal dividends of the additional growth (Takizawa, Gardner, and Ueda 2004).

Modified versions of the PIH model can be designed to incorporate the scaling up of public investment and allow a more front-loaded spending path financed by resource revenue. Models may assume, as a "worst-case scenario," that the scaling up of public investment does not have an impact on growth. Or it may be assumed that higher public investment has a favorable effect on growth, which would generate higher nonresource revenues, but also higher operations and maintenance costs for the additional public capital. IMF (2012a, 2015a) and Baunsgaard and others (2012) discuss modified PIH approaches with scaled-up capital spending. They also provide practical examples of how such approaches can be implemented. Box 4.1 provides some examples of World Bank advice.

Box 4.1. Fiscal Frameworks and Sustainability in Resource-Rich Countries: Examples of World Bank Advice

In its work with countries, the World Bank has recommended the introduction of fiscal frameworks incorporating stabilization and sustainability objectives, tailored to specific country circumstances. Examples include Kazakhstan, the Lao People's Democratic Republic (PDR), and Mozambique.

In Kazakhstan, the Bank advocated a fiscal framework focused on a fiscal rule for the non-oil deficit consistent with intergenerational equity and a resource fund integrated with the rule. The framework is based on a permanent-income approach and also includes a countercyclical component (Eckardt, Sarsenov, and Thomas 2012).

box continues next page

Box 4.1 Fiscal Frameworks and Sustainability in Resource-Rich Countries: Examples of World Bank Advice (continued)

In Lao PDR, the Bank saw the conduct of a fiscal policy that explicitly accounts for exhaustible resource revenues as a way to reduce harmful impacts and volatility (World Bank 2010a). It simulated various fiscal strategies to estimate future trajectories of public debt and public financial assets, and subjected the results to sensitivity analyses.

In Mozambique, the Bank advised the adoption of a fiscal sustainability framework (FSF) that would provide for increasing public investment in line with capacity constraints to accelerate growth in the nonresource sector and meet development needs (World Bank 2014a). The Bank cautioned, however, that the extent to which the FSF would achieve higher growth would depend on the quality of public expenditure. In this regard, it saw continued progress in public financial management (PFM) reforms, and improvement in the public investment management (PIM) system, as crucial to generate the expected returns and to ensure that increased public spending delivers the expected results. The Bank simulated potential revenues from the resource sector over a 20-year period, with a frontloading of public investments, and fiscal rules limiting public expenditure growth (to address revenue volatility and expenditure capacity constraints). It also generated projections for public savings and the accumulation of financial assets.

Source: Authors, based on sources noted in box.

Will public investment generate fiscal revenues and preserve fiscal sustainability? If the net fiscal return on the scaled-up investment is larger than the foregone return on net financial assets, net government wealth after the scaling up of investment could be higher than in the absence of such investment. But this will depend on whether the expenditures have a positive impact on growth, and on whether the government can reap fiscal dividends from that growth. Fiscal dividends include tax revenue from greater economic activity and higher user fees, if applicable.

Sustained growth benefits will come about if public investment is productive. Poor governance, defective public investment systems, and supply bottlenecks may impair the productivity of investment. Ramping up public investment in these circumstances could run into inefficiencies, hamper the transformation of natural resources into productive public capital, and, rather than contributing to sustained growth, could result in a waste of resources. Fast increases in investment could also increase macroeconomic instability and vulnerability to shocks, and generate currency appreciation or "Dutch disease" effects—all of which can affect long-term growth.

Growth, in turn, will lead to higher fiscal revenues if the higher potential revenue base is taxed and the revenues collected, and if the financial returns cover the future running costs of the projects. The government must be able to capture returns on investment adequate to finance the future operation, maintenance, and depreciation costs associated with the completed projects. The financial returns have to cover these additional recurrent costs to have a positive impact on the government's cash flow, and therefore on sustainability.

If the higher revenue base is given away (through tax holidays, tax incentives, exemptions, tax-free zones, and the like), not taxed appropriately (as in the case of the weak nonresource tax systems seen in many low-income, resource-rich countries), or not collected because of weaknesses in revenue administration agencies, growth may not generate fiscal dividends. In such cases, the higher public investment expenditure could affect fiscal sustainability.

Probabilistic approaches to sustainability analyses would be appropriate given the magnitude of the risks and uncertainties surrounding the projections, if adequate capacity exists. For example, Celasun, Debrun, and Ostry (2006) use a probabilistic (fan chart) approach to analyze debt sustainability.

Estimates of public sector net worth and sustainability can in resource-rich countries be very volatile, due to the volatility of key parameters such as resource and input prices. For example, for a number of countries estimated government net worth was revised sharply down in 2015 as oil prices dropped and the value of oil reserves fell.

Finally, uncertainty rises the longer the projection period, and the uncertainties surrounding long-term sustainability exercises are enormous. Estimates of wealth from future resource revenue are subject to uncertainty about many factors, including future resource prices and production costs, the size of resource reserves in the ground, the fiscal regime applied to the resource sector, and interest rates. Given these uncertainties and the asymmetric penalty function mentioned above (Gelb and Garsmann 2010), it would be advisable for long-term sustainability exercises to include an element of caution and prudence.

Adjusted Net Saving Models

Under the "wealth of nations" approach, a country's total wealth—including produced, natural, and intangible (human and institutional) capital—is estimated. Changes in wealth are tracked as a key indicator of sustainability. Empirical wealth estimates produced by the World Bank suggest that the preponderant form of wealth worldwide is intangible capital, that is, human capital and the quality of formal and informal institutions (World Bank 2006a, 2011). The share of natural capital in total wealth tends to fall with income, while the share of intangible capital rises. In LICs natural capital (including nonrenewable resources) is a significant portion of total wealth, and is on average greater than the share of produced capital.

Natural capital can be transformed into other forms of capital, provided resource rents are effectively and efficiently invested.[6] Natural rents can be an important source of development, and some countries have successfully used natural resources in this way, including by diversifying their economies away from heavy dependence on resources or by preparing for these resources' eventual depletion.

A key concept relevant to the preservation of wealth is adjusted net savings. In resource-rich countries resource dependence complicates the measurement of savings and consumption, because the depletion of natural resources is not visible in the standard national or fiscal accounts. Adjusted net or genuine savings constitute an attempt to measure the true level of savings in a country after the depletion of minerals, energy, and forests; the depreciation of produced capital; investment in human capital (as measured by education expenditure); and environmental damage. Sustained negative adjusted savings would lead to lower national wealth and diminished social welfare.

World Bank research suggests that many resource-rich countries, especially in Sub-Saharan Africa, display very low or negative adjusted net savings, including in recent boom times. In 2008 a group of 21 oil- and gas-exporting countries were estimated to have had negative adjusted net savings on average (Ross, Kaiser, and Mazaheri 2011).[7]

Appropriate policies are needed to revert negative net adjusted savings trends. In particular, resource-rich countries will benefit from macroeconomic policies that encourage saving, resource policies that lead to dynamically efficient rates of extraction, fiscal regimes that capture resource rents, and public investment programs that put resource revenues to their best use, including investment in human capital (Hamilton and Ley 2010).

Notes

1. Some countries are resource rich, but because of the development of their nonresource sectors, the latter contribute significant tax revenues. Thus, fiscal resource dependence in these countries has declined over time.

2. See Halland, Lokanc, and Nair (2015) for a discussion of reserves.

3. Traditional debt-sustainability analyses (DSAs) in non-resource-rich countries incorporate intertemporal welfare choices implicitly, for example, by recommending that the ratio of debt to gross domestic product (GDP) be stabilized at a "prudent" level. This recommendation has fundamental implications for the assignment of debt repayment responsibilities between current and future generations—implications that are rarely made explicit.

4. See IMF (2012a) and Baunsgaard and others (2012) for an in-depth discussion of the issues.

5. It should be noted that the standard DSAs of emerging markets and developed economies also rely on the primary balance, and also rarely distinguish between public consumption and investment.

6. Hartwick's rule proposes a concept of sustainability in resource-rich countries: if the value of investment in productive capital offsets declining stocks of exhaustible resources, a constant level of consumption can be sustained.

7. For example, after adjusting net national income for the depletion of natural resources, Ley (2010) finds that Zambia had very low, and often negative, rates of adjusted savings, implying declining national wealth. An earlier study by Lange (2004) finds similar results for Namibia, while it finds that Botswana has managed to use its natural capital to build national wealth.

CHAPTER 5

Public Financial Management, Public Investment Management, and Fiscal Transparency

Public Financial Management Systems and Governance

The effectiveness and efficiency of public expenditure is particularly important for resource-rich countries, where spending is partly financed by temporary revenues from exhaustible resources, which puts a premium on their good and careful use. It is also critical for sustainable and inclusive growth and poverty reduction (World Bank 2006b).

A number of resource-rich countries have significantly improved the quality of their institutions and budget management, including their capacity to manage the planning, allocation, and effective control of budgetary resources. These countries have improved their institutional ratings (as measured by World Bank governance indicators in the past decade). In other resource-rich countries, however, progress has been mixed. In some of these countries the budget systems suffer from important weaknesses and the quality and efficiency of spending are in need of substantive enhancement. And in many of these countries, large increases in expenditure in recent years—facilitated by the resource price boom—have put additional pressures on public financial management (PFM) systems.

Governance problems can be an important factor preventing the improvement of budgetary institutions, which in turn hampers the ability to turn resource wealth into sustainable development. Governance challenges can trump economic challenges, whose technical solutions are well known (IMF 2010a). In the natural resource value chain, key actors in the distribution of rents (through current spending and investment) include the ministry of finance (MoF), sector agencies, contractors, and beneficiaries (Barma and others 2012). In particular, the availability of resource revenue can reduce pressures for accountability. It can also provide incentives to use resources inappropriately, which is helped by deficient fiscal reporting and insufficient transparency. This, in turn, can discourage the drive for improvements in PFM and fiscal transparency (see, for example, Isham and others 2005; Mehlum, Moene, and Torvik 2006; Collier and others 2009; Barma and others 2012).

Large increases in spending can be associated with political economy and governance issues. Politicians may raise public spending and employment excessively and too rapidly, with the aim of increasing their patronage networks and improving their chances of staying in power, while resources shift out of productive activity into unproductive rent-seeking activity (Mehlum, Moene, and Torvik 2006; Brahmbhatt and Canuto 2010).

Resource exporters tend to have weaker budget institutions than other countries at similar levels of development, as shown by indicators of governance and quality of expenditure. For example, Dabla-Norris and others (2010), in a study of multidimensional indices of the quality of budget institutions in low-income countries (LICs), find that oil exporters have the weakest budget institutions across all dimensions (see also World Bank 2010b; Akitoby and Coorey 2012). This has fundamental implications for the effectiveness and efficiency of public spending, including the ability of public investment to contribute to sustainable growth.

For example, in Mozambique, the World Bank noted that despite impressive progress on PFM reforms, the country would need to further strengthen PFM in key areas for managing resource revenues, particularly in light of the expected surge in resource (coal and gas) revenues. It provided detailed recommendations for improvements in budget presentation; medium-term planning and budgeting; budget execution, cash flow, and budgetary credibility; comprehensiveness and transparency; and external accountability. The Bank emphasized that the quality of governance, the transparency of PFM, and the integrity of public institutions are key elements in the relationship between resource revenues and long-term growth (World Bank 2014a).

The rapid growth of public spending during the resource boom has increased the urgency of strengthening PFM systems and fiscal transparency in many resource-rich countries to put time-bound resources to good use. There is also a need for intensified scrutiny of the quality of expenditure and its efficiency. To ensure efficiency and value for money, governments need to undertake and report periodic reviews of the quality of stepped-up spending.

Depending on specific country circumstances, desirable PFM reforms may be required in areas such as the fiscal legal framework, budget formulation, budget presentation, medium- and long-term fiscal planning, budget execution, audit and reporting.[1]

Public Investment Management Systems

The impact of public investment, and particularly infrastructure investment, on growth has attracted a lot of research interest. In developing countries, low stocks of infrastructure assets are often a constraint on growth. A majority of studies find positive effects of public capital on output and growth (Servén

2007; Calderón and Servén 2014). In particular, a recent study finds that infrastructure development has positive effects on income growth and, more tentatively, on distributive equity (Calderón and Servén 2014). Empirical evidence points to the high returns and positive externalities due to public infrastructure (World Bank 2006b).[2]

This said, the quality of public investment is critical for its payoff in terms of economic growth. Econometric evidence suggests that the quality of public investment, as measured by variables capturing the adequacy of project selection and implementation, is statistically significant in explaining variations in growth, a result driven mainly by LICs (Gupta and others 2014).

Resource-rich countries face the challenge of turning resource wealth in the ground into productive assets. Public investment is key to realizing the potential developmental contribution of extractive industries to broad-based growth and improved social welfare (Rajaram and others 2014).

Weaknesses in public investment can undermine one of the primary arguments for higher investment: that it can enhance future economic prospects. Developing resource-rich countries tend to have weaker public investment management (PIM) systems than other countries at similar levels of development. Evidence is provided, for example, in the following three studies:

- A recent World Bank study of PIM found that developing resource-rich countries consistently fall short in terms of the quality and quantity of their capital spending, owing to capacity and political constraints (Rajaram and others 2014). In particular, the study notes that governments dependent on resource revenue face a number of generic and specific challenges to improving public investment:
  - Revenue volatility and "boom and bust" cycles
  - Public investment through a variety of modalities beyond traditional budget financing
  - Overly large public investment relative to the size of the economy (which can create congestion and crowding effects)
  - The rapid scaling up and cutting back of capital spending (which often takes place in resource-dependent settings)
- In a comprehensive study, Dabla-Norris and others (2011) examine public investment efficiency using an index of the institutional environment supporting PIM across four stages of the investment process: project appraisal, selection, implementation, and evaluation. Their data suggest that, on average, oil exporters have lower scores than other countries in their sample. To put this in context, Gupta and others (2014) find that in a sample of 52 developing countries, on average only about half of public investment effort translates into actual productive public capital, although there is significant heterogeneity across the sample.
- A study of public investment in oil-exporting countries (OECs) in the Middle East and North Africa (MENA) region and in the Caucasus and Central Asia

region found that these countries appear to lag behind the best performers on all three main public investment efficiency measures used in the study, and have substantial room to improve public investment effciency. The study also found that strong institutions can play a crucial role in fostering the efficiency of public investment (Albino-War and others 2014).

Procyclical fiscal policies in a number of resource-rich countries, as discussed in chapter 2, have affected public investment through "stop and go" dynamics. The quality of public investment can be affected in upswings as well as in downswings.

Rising or elevated resource prices often lead to booms in public investment that place PIM systems under pressure. A number of indicators may signal the deteriorating quality of investment spending:

- The criteria for the selection and prioritization of capital projects become lax.
- Implementation bottlenecks and delays arise as capacity in the construction sector and other nontraded sectors is stretched.
- As noted earlier, the costs faced by the public sector increase when supply bottlenecks occur if the private sector is booming.

When resource prices fall and fiscal positions come under pressure, public investment often suffers. Public investment is a discretionary form of spending, and thus typically more prone to cuts than current expenditures, such as the wage bill or transfer programs—areas where cuts often meet with strong opposition (Barma and others 2012). International evidence suggests that reductions in infrastructure spending often account for a large share of fiscal deficit reductions (Easterly, Irwin, and Servén 2008), and there is strong evidence from Latin America, Africa, and South Asia that public capital formation was the government spending category that suffered the greatest reductions at times of fiscal stabilization (World Bank 2006b). Evidence from fiscal adjustments undertaken by a number of countries through the 1990s also suggests that cutbacks in public investment contributed to declines in economic growth and that, from an intertemporal perspective, this may have been a suboptimal design of fiscal policy (Easterly, Irwin, and Servén 2008; Rajaram and others 2014).

As a result of these approaches, projects are slowed down or paralyzed, and sometimes the operating costs of completed projects cannot be met. The volatility of capital expenditure creates uncertainty among contractors and suppliers. Fluctuations in public investment make cash flows to contractors volatile and unpredictable, and disrupt regular maintenance, which contributes to inefficiency. Volatile capital budgets also create problems of credibility when negotiating public contracts, and contractors looking at past government practices may seek "insurance" in the form of higher prices charged to the public sector.

Against this background, the World Bank (2006a, 2007) has noted the importance of protecting public investment in the context of fiscal adjustments. Taking into account the evidence that the quality of fiscal adjustment has implications for growth, the Bank has proposed ways in which fiscal policy might be designed to promote growth and development while preserving macroeconomic stability. Some general principles apply: Cuts in public consumption are generally preferable to cuts in public investment. Also, reallocating resources from less efficient to more productive uses is likely to better enhance long-term growth, other things being equal, than raising additional revenue or borrowing to finance the same productive expenditure.

Rajaram and others (2010, 2014) and Rajaram (2012) provide a pragmatic and objective diagnostic approach to the assessment of PIM systems for governments (figure 5.1). The framework identifies eight key "must have" stages of a well-functioning public investment system, and proposes practical diagnostics (not reported here) to assess them.

For example, in Mozambique a recent World Bank report found that PIM capacity is relatively weak, and highlighted that project appraisal (stage 2 in figure 5.1) in particular scored well below the average of comparable countries (World Bank 2014a). Given that appraisal processes are critical to select projects with high economic and social returns, the report notes that reforms to improve the quality of project preparation and appraisal could improve significantly the value-for-money of public investments. But sustained improvement would also be needed in other aspects of the PIM system.

Frameworks that take macroeconomic and capacity constraints into account when calibrating how fast to scale up investment have been developed. For

Figure 5.1. Diagnostic Framework for Assessing Public Investment Management

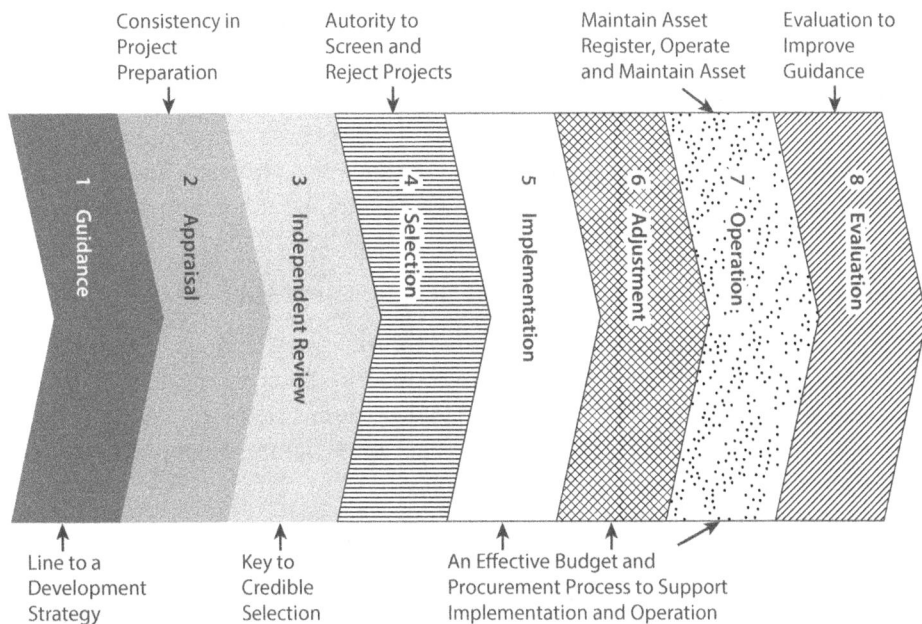

Source: Rajaram (2012).

Box 5.1 The Sustainable Investing Approach

The sustainable investing approach (SIA) takes into account important features common in developing countries, including inefficient public investment, institutional and absorptive capacity constraints, weak tax systems, and "Dutch disease" (Berg and others 2012). It proposes raising public investment gradually in line with institutional and absorptive capacity constraints, and saving some of the resources.

The SIA incorporates quantitative measures of investment efficiency explicitly in the framework. This includes a feature observed in developing countries: if public investment is scaled up quickly (as often observed during resource windfalls), capacity constraints due to factors such as supply bottlenecks or poor planning can drive up investment costs. Indeed, indirect evidence suggests a declining return on investment as the latter accelerates. The SIA also accounts for the fiscal costs of operating and preserving public capital.

The gradual scaling up of public investment gives governments time to improve public investment efficiency. It also allows for building buffers to prevent damaging disruptions to public investment in the event of negative resource shocks.

Berg and others (2012) stress the importance of assessing both the rate of return of public investment projects and absorptive capacity constraints. They also emphasize that the financing of the projects' future recurrent costs should be accounted for, so that the growth benefits of public investment can be sustained.[3]

Source: Berg and others (2012).

---

example, to address the potential problems discussed, Berg and others (2012) propose a "sustainable investing approach" (SIA). This framework can help determine how much and how fast public investment may be scaled up, with the aim to transform a portion of resource wealth into public capital—that can in turn increase the productivity of private activities while maintaining economic stability. The SIA explicitly accounts for the investment inefficiency and absorptive capacity constraints often found in developing resource-rich countries (box 5.1).

Capacity Issues in New and Prospective Resource Producers

New and prospective resource producers face the issue that resource revenues can increase much faster than the government's ability to spend them effectively and efficiently. It takes time to build government absorptive capacity. In addition, in these countries the public sector often competes with large private resource companies for scarce human skills.

Some low-income prospective producers face the challenge of transitioning from reliance on foreign aid to reliance, or greater reliance, on resource revenues. In some of these countries, PIM capacity may be limited because much of the public investment was concessionally financed by multilateral institutions or bilateral agencies that have their own appraisal and evaluation mechanisms, and that supported project implementation. As the prospect of resource revenues materializes, this may change rapidly—faster than the government can set up or improve the institutions to design, appraise, select, implement, and evaluate public investment projects.

In these countries, therefore, saving part of the early resource revenues is advisable not only because of the macroeconomic stability and fiscal risk considerations discussed above, but also—and perhaps equally importantly—because of the government's possible inability, in the short run, to use the additional resources effectively due to institutional and capacity constraints. Thus, for example, Collier has argued that a critical stage prior to an increase in domestic investment is to build the capacity to manage it: "investing in investing" (Collier 2012). Technical assistance in capacity building can help these countries gradually lift the capacity constraint.

Fiscal Transparency

A substantial empirical literature supports the proposition that fiscal transparency is beneficial by several different criteria (Heald 2013; De Renzio and Wehner 2015). Transparency and accountability—that is, the obligation or willingness to accept responsibility or to account for one's actions—are vital for the efficient functioning of the economy and for fostering growth and social inclusion. They are critical in establishing and preserving credibility in the management of resource revenue (Barma and others 2012).

The existence of large rents and revenues that do not arise from domestic taxation make resource-rich countries especially vulnerable and prone to problems in these areas. Empirical evidence suggests that lack of transparency and of institutional controls are the main factors behind corruption in expenditure, for instance, in public investment and procurement. While weak transparency and governance are not circumscribed to resource-rich countries, the potential costs of lack of transparent practices are substantial in these countries. Institutional strengthening to improve transparency, therefore, promises ample rewards (Carstens 2005; IMF 2007a).

Poor economic management and rent seeking can be viewed as an agency problem. There may be diverging interests and asymmetric information between the principal (representing the public interest) and the public agency (Dabla-Norris and Paul 2006).

Transparency can reduce the agency problem. Information can contribute to reduced rent capture, and to higher public output and productivity. The availability of information about the agent makes the agent more accountable to the principal. Also, transparency strengthens decision making. It ensures that information is available to identify weaknesses, define policy responses, measure the government's performance, and guard against possible misuse of power. This in turn furthers accountability.

The International Monetary Fund's (IMF's) Fiscal Transparency Code identifies important transparency principles and practices and provides desirable standards for the disclosure of information about public finances. Following such recommendations can help ensure public access to a clear picture of the structure and finances of the government,[4] and help all stakeholders reliably assess the soundness of fiscal policy. The code has four pillars: (i) fiscal reporting, (ii) fiscal forecasting and budgeting, (iii) fiscal risk analysis and management, and (iv) resource revenue management. The draft resource revenue management pillar puts forth proposed fiscal transparency principles and practices for each stage of the resource revenue management process for resource-rich countries.[5]

Notes

1. Dabán and Hélis (2013) discuss a number of PFM issues in resource-rich countries, and offer suggestions for well-designed and sequenced reforms.

2. The marginal productivity of infrastructure investment and maintenance is high when such investments are effectively implemented. For example, Estache and Liu (2003, cited in World Bank 2006b) estimate social rates of return on World Bank infrastructure projects in excess of 20 percent for telecommunications, transport, and urban projects over 1964–2003. Another World Bank study finds that infrastructure contributed significantly to Africa's improved growth performance in the 2000s (Foster and Briceño-Garmendia 2010).

3. The authors illustrate the sustainable investing approach (SIA) by calibrating it to the Central African Economic and Monetary Community (CEMAC) region and to Angola, and simulating future fiscal and macroeconomic paths.

4. blog-pfm.imf.org/files/ft-code.pdf.

5. The pillar was open to public comment (www.imf.org/np/exr/consult/2014/ftc/pdf/121814.pdf). It will replace the IMF's earlier *Guide on Resource Revenue Transparency* (IMF 2007a). A summary of the fiscal transparency practices for resource revenue management set forth in the IMF (2007a) guide can be found in appendix F.

PART III

Special Fiscal Institutions in Resource-Rich Countries

CHAPTER 6

Medium-Term Expenditure Frameworks

A medium-term perspective on annual budgeting is essential. It is vitally important to introduce an awareness of the future—beyond the budget year—into the budgeting system, and provide for a more informed and systematic discussion of fiscal and public spending strategies. The enhancement of the links between annual budgets and medium- and long-term fiscal objectives, and the introduction of assessments of fiscal risks, can help (i) improve fiscal management and the allocation of public resources, and (ii) address short-term policy bias and tendencies toward procyclicality that increase fiscal vulnerabilities in many resource-rich countries.

A medium-term expenditure framework (MTEF) can be an important component of a comprehensive fiscal framework. Crucially, a well-developed MTEF addresses what is arguably one of the most important causes of poor budgeting outcomes in developing countries: the failure to link policy, planning, and budgeting (World Bank 1998).[1]

In resource-rich countries in particular, an MTEF can help link annual budgets to longer-term policies and fiscal sustainability objectives. It can enhance fiscal risk analysis in the face of revenue volatility. And it can provide an institutional framework for addressing medium- and long-term resource allocation issues in the presence of resource revenue.

MTEFs in resource-rich countries help meet objectives that traditional one-year incremental budgeting does not reliably meet. In particular, they can:

- Promote fiscal discipline so that spending is sustainable, limited by resource availability, and does not generate excessive fiscal vulnerabilities going forward.
- Ensure that budget allocations reflect expenditure priorities as set out in medium-term policies.

- Provide an institutional framework to assess fiscal sustainability issues and take them into account in the framing of fiscal strategies.
- Promote transparency, a more informed public discussion, governance, and accountability.

There are three main forms of MTEFs, and these involve increasing levels of complexity and demands on capacity. The World Bank (2012) identifies the following frameworks:

- The simplest MTEF is a medium-term fiscal framework (MTFF). It entails a statement of fiscal policy objectives; a macro-fiscal strategy; integrated medium-term macroeconomic projections within which the annual budget and multiyear budget estimates can be presented and discussed; fiscal targets, rolling aggregate revenue, expenditure, and other fiscal forecasts; and fiscal risk and sustainability analysis.
- A medium-term budget framework (MTBF) includes, in addition, the bottom-up determination of spending agency resource needs, and reconciliation of these with the resource envelope.
- A medium-term performance framework (MTPF) includes sector objectives and strategies, including specific agency and/or program output or outcome targets, with an emphasis on the measurement and evaluation of performance.

MTEFs are not multiyear budgets and do not introduce rigidity. At first glance, it might seem that MTEFs would be at odds with the budget flexibility that resource-rich countries need in the face of substantial revenue volatility. It might be thought that MTEFs will set in stone rigid fiscal and spending plans, when budgets in resource-rich countries need flexibility to react to unforeseen developments in resource prices and other shocks. However, an MTEF is not a multiyear budget (Schiavo-Campo 2007). Expenditure ceilings for the years beyond the initial annual budget tend to be no more than indicative. Unanticipated developments and large deviations from MTEF projections in later years can be assessed and addressed through adjustments to the MTEF when circumstances warrant it. Far from introducing rigidity, by extending the planning horizon, MTEFs adapted to the circumstances faced by resource-rich countries are a useful tool for fiscal management in these countries.

A comprehensive study finds evidence of the positive impact of MTEFs (World Bank 2012). The study uses various methodological approaches that include event studies, econometric analysis, and country case studies to assess the effect of MTEFs on achieving three objectives: fiscal discipline, allocative efficiency, and technical efficiency. The evidence indicates that all types of MTFF have a robust and significant positive impact on fiscal discipline. There is also evidence that MTEFs improve allocative efficiency, while the results on technical efficiency are more mixed. The case study analyses indicate that MTEFs improve fiscal discipline, make budgeting more strategic, improve the recognition of resource constraints, and foster cooperation among government agencies. Improvements in spending efficiency are less clear, although spending in targeted sectors increased.

The implementation of MTEFs must be gradual and consistent with capacity. Brumby and Hemming (2013) contrast the broadly positive experience of Uganda, where an MTBF was implemented years after the introduction of an MTFF, with the negative experience of Ghana in the late 1990s—the country moved straight into an MTBF with MTPF elements without being ready for anything more than an MTFF.

The rest of this chapter focuses on the role MTEFs can play in helping quantify and manage fiscal risks and long-term sustainability issues in resource-rich countries.

Medium-Term Expenditure Frameworks and Fiscal Risks

As discussed above, in resource-rich countries the volatility and uncertainty of resource revenues is a key source of fiscal risk. Other sources of fiscal risk are macroeconomic (such as those arising from unexpected fluctuations in interest rates and exchange rates) and those associated with contingent government expenditures, public enterprises, subnational governments (SNGs), public-private partnerships (PPPs), the financial system, and natural disasters (Cebotari and others 2009).

Resource-rich countries that have passed legislation on the disclosure of fiscal risks or contingent liabilities include Australia, Canada, Chile, Colombia, Nigeria, and Peru. As of 2009 seven countries (including some nonrenewable resource exporters) consolidated information on fiscal risks in a single published document (Australia, Brazil, Chile, Colombia, Indonesia, New Zealand, and Pakistan) (Everaert and others 2009).

MTEFs can be specifically designed to help quantify and address fiscal risks. In resource-rich countries where fiscal policies continue to focus on one-year budgets with little reference to fiscal risks and vulnerabilities, there is a need to focus more on resource revenue volatility and uncertainty in the medium term. An MTEF is particularly important when revenues fluctuate significantly and unpredictably. The MTEF would benefit from the inclusion of strategies to address fiscal risks and vulnerabilities, and from the formulation of mitigating fiscal strategies (as discussed in chapter 3). Capacity permitting, the MTEF would contain a broad fiscal risk statement.

Information and discussion on resource-revenue-related risks—and the enhancement of transparency—promote informed analysis and scrutiny of fiscal strategies and their implications for risk. From a political economy point of view, this can help build support for prudent and less procyclical fiscal policies in the face of resource revenue volatility. The public scrutiny that comes with quantification and disclosure can create pressure to ensure that risks are contained and appropriately managed. Politicians and legislatures may be less enthusiastic about supporting risky spending increases during booms, if they and the public are provided with a clear statement of what this would imply in terms of fiscal vulnerability to resource price downturns, and the kind of fiscal adjustments that would be required if such a situation arose.

Medium-Term Expenditure Frameworks and Long-Term Perspectives for Fiscal Policy

In many resource-rich countries there is a need for technical analyses and wider political debates to span longer horizons (Eifert, Gelb, and Tallroth 2003). In some resource-rich countries with large nonresource deficits and public debt, the expected resource production horizon at current output rates is not long, but policies continue to be carried out as if those resources were of infinite duration. In countries where fiscal discussion is excessively or exclusively focused on the short term, the development of institutions that promote a long-term perspective can help moderate procyclicality, and focus public attention on strategic issues relevant to resource use. This is also warranted given the inability of future generations to voice preferences on the issues at hand today.

Comparing temporary resource rents to long-run pressures on public finances—such as future increases in age- and health-related spending, social spending, environmental costs, contingent liabilities, and debt service—would contribute to an informed political discussion of the budget in a longer-term perspective. It could dampen resource euphoria and promote fiscal prudence.

For example, a simple graph showing declining net cash flows from the oil sector and mounting pension pressures in the long term was widely used in Norway at the time of the introduction of fiscal guidelines in 2001 (figure 6.1).

Figure 6.1 Norway: Net Cash Flow from the Petroleum Sector and Pension Expenditures (2001 Projections)

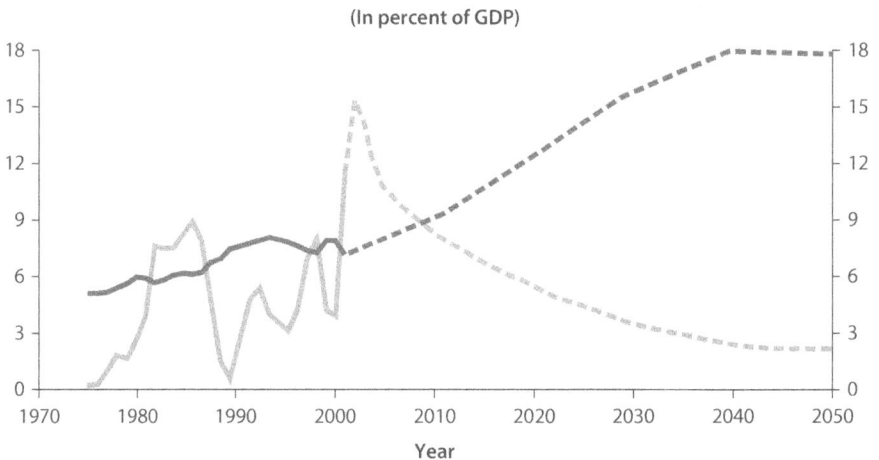

Source: Skancke 2003.
Note: GDP = gross domestic product.

It helped build broad political and social support for a prudent and sustainable fiscal policy and the institutional frameworks supporting it. In the years after the graph was developed, it became a standard feature of fiscal policy documents in Norway and was widely understood by the population (Skancke 2003).

MTEFs with extensive risk and long-term analyses also bring out acute policy trade-offs that are seldom considered explicitly. For example:

- In the short term and in the face of an increase in resource prices, what is the trade-off between increasing expenditure and raising fiscal risks?
- From a long-run perspective, what are the trade-offs between accumulating physical capital as opposed to net financial assets?
- What are the trade-offs between increasing public consumption against the expected value of future net assets when the resource runs out?

MTEFs require adaptation to planning uncertainty. Long-term planning is subject to considerable uncertainty: measures of sustainable public spending may vary over time, and estimates of long-term spending pressures may change as circumstances change. A rolling MTEF that is updated as circumstances change and new information comes in helps clarify how policy choices relate to immediate and longer-term objectives, and their likely consequences.

Progress in the implementation of MTEFs in resource-rich countries has been uneven. For example, as of 2011 only five of the thirteen Middle East and North Africa (MENA) oil and gas exporters had a formal or functionally equivalent MTFF, and only one had an MTBF (Ross, Kaiser, and Mazaheri 2011). In Latin America, several resource exporters have implemented MTEFs, including Chile, Colombia, Mexico, and Peru.

Several resource-rich countries have implemented or are moving toward adopting at least basic forms of MTEFs that include fiscal risk and long-term analyses. Box 6.1 provides some examples.

Box 6.1 Medium-Term Expenditure Frameworks and Fiscal Risk and Long-Term Analyses in Resource-Rich Countries

Colombia's 2013 medium-term framework (MTF) included risk analysis of the public debt, a statement of quasi-fiscal activities, costing of the long-term implications of laws enacted in the previous year, and extensive costing of implicit and contingent liabilities (Colombia 2013).

Nigeria's 2014–16 medium-term expenditure framework (MTEF) and Fiscal Strategy Paper included a brief discussion of the impact of fiscal shock scenarios such as a global economic downturn, falling oil prices, and risks to oil production and non-oil revenue (Nigeria 2014).

---

box continues next page

Box 6.1 Medium-Term Expenditure Frameworks and Fiscal Risk and Long-Term Analyses in Resource-Rich Countries *(continued)*

Budget documents in Norway contain a statement on medium-term fiscal policy objectives and comprehensive discussions of long-term fiscal sustainability and fiscal risks. A paper on long-term perspectives for the Norwegian economy is produced every four years (see, for example, Norway 2013).

The 2015–17 MTF in Peru includes a comprehensive debt-sustainability analysis (DSA) with a 10-year horizon (including a stochastic DSA) and a sensitivity analysis and stress test of the fiscal position in the medium term (Peru 2014). The sensitivity analysis considers two potential external shocks—a deterioration in the terms of trade associated with a strong deceleration of the growth rate in China or a rapid tapering of monetary impulse in the United States and higher perception of risk in emerging market economies—and an internal shock (a strong "El Niño"). It quantifies the impact of those risks, if they were to materialize, on the balance of payments, the domestic economy, and the fiscal accounts. The analysis also assesses the capacity to undertake a countercyclical fiscal policy as a mitigation strategy in case of a significant economic downturn, which might involve invoking the exceptional escape clause in the structural fiscal rule.

The Russian Federation introduced a medium-term fiscal framework (MTFF) with rolling three-year budget plans that incorporate the non-oil balance as a key fiscal concept and explicit long-term budget planning, modeled on New Zealand's and Australia's practices. The framework's relevance has been limited, however, because it has not been used as a credible MTEF, as medium-term expenditure forecasts have been weak. In addition, excessive use of almost invariably procyclical supplementary budgets undermined the MTFF (Gust and Zakharova 2012).

Timor-Leste, despite severe administrative capacity limitations, adopted a fiscal framework based on the estimated sustainable income (ESI) from oil wealth in the long term. The government budget documents include detailed sensitivity analyses of the impact on the ESI of changes in key long-term assumptions. The ESI is stress tested for lower oil prices, lower oil and gas production, and higher production costs (World Bank 2013b; Timor-Leste 2014).

Source: Authors, based on sources noted in box.

Factors for the Success of Medium-Term Expenditure Frameworks

While experience with MTEFs around the world is varied and general lessons are hard to draw, the evidence points to a few key factors that might contribute to these frameworks' success in resource-rich countries:

- *Gradualism and the right sequencing.* It is important to avoid moving too fast. Countries can start with the basics (such as a simple aggregate MTFF), and only gradually move on to more demanding MTBFs—but the specificity of resource revenue is best incorporated into the structure of the MTFF from the very beginning. The very demanding technical and institutional requirements for MTPFs suggest the need for substantial experience and success with an MTBF before an MTPF can be considered.

- *Political commitment at high levels—including buy in from the ministry of finance (MoF)—to a comprehensive and realistic budget process.* In some resource-rich countries the political economy of spending resource rents will be against the introduction or strengthening of an MTEF because of the vested interests and powerful constituencies that might be affected by greater transparency in policy choices and budget processes. In such cases, support from the top is key.
- *Ability to realistically forecast key fiscal aggregates,* which in turn allows the clear articulation of fiscal policy objectives and targets. Resource revenue poses a particularly difficult challenge, which can be addressed with strategies that are discussed later in this volume and the risk analysis mechanisms noted above.
- *Integration of the MTEF with the budget process and national/sectorial strategies.* This is particularly important in resource-rich countries that retain separate fiscal institutions that plan and execute investment, often not fully coordinated with the budget, as well as extrabudgetary funds and resource funds with authority to spend.
- *A strong coordinating agency,* typically the MoF, with inclusive participation of other agencies.
- *Accountability for budget discipline,* with robust systems of budget execution and reporting.
- *A commitment to publicity and dissemination,* to strengthen political and public support for the MTEF.

Note

1. Medium-term expenditure frameworks (MTEFs) have been discussed at length in other World Bank and International Monetary Fund (IMF) documents. See, in particular, World Bank (2012) and various entries in the IMF Public Financial Management (PFM) blog (blog-pfm.imf.org/pfmblog/).

CHAPTER 7

Fiscal Rules and Fiscal Councils

Fiscal Rules

Fiscal rules are defined as standing commitments to specified numerical targets or ceilings for some key budget aggregates. Unlike fiscal rules, fiscal guidelines are not legally binding.[1]

In resource-rich countries fiscal rules or guidelines are often motivated by a desire to reduce the procyclicality of fiscal policy in the face of volatile resource revenue, and to promote savings and sustainability. Often, fiscal rules have been motivated by political economy factors: they have been seen as potentially useful instruments to address spending pressures or to enhance the credibility of the government.

Fiscal rules are less common than resource funds in resource-rich countries. However, they can play a more critical role because, unlike resource funds, they are intended to constrain fiscal policy directly.

In resource-rich countries the design of appropriate fiscal rules is more challenging than in other countries. The characteristics of resource revenue—highly volatile and uncertain, dependent on exhaustible resources, and largely originating from abroad—greatly complicate the design of fiscal rules. Other factors, such as revenue sharing in federal states and resource revenue earmarking, can also complicate the design and implementation of fiscal rules in these countries (see, for example, Cueva 2008). Therefore, as discussed below, some types of fiscal rules found in other countries are not applicable in resource-rich countries, particularly in those heavily dependent on resource revenue.

The use of fiscal rules and guidelines in resource-rich countries has been relatively limited. Their design has varied greatly. Some countries have targeted a single fiscal indicator, while others have targeted two or more indicators. The following fiscal indicators have been targeted[2]: overall balance (for example, the Canadian province of Alberta, Indonesia, Mexico, Nigeria, Peru); current balance (República Bolivariana de Venezuela); structural balance (SB), with estimated "structural" resource revenue (Chile, Colombia, Mongolia, Peru); nonresource balance (NRB) (Ecuador, the Russian Federation, Timor-Leste);

nonresource current balance (Ecuador, Equatorial Guinea); structural NRB (Norway); rate of growth or level of expenditure or of components of expenditure (Botswana, Chad, Ecuador, Mexico, Mongolia, Peru, Russia, República Bolivariana de Venezuela); and the ratio of public debt to gross domestic product (GDP) (Alberta, Ecuador, Mongolia, República Bolivariana de Venezuela).[3] Some resource-rich countries have implemented fiscal rules in conjunction with resource funds.

The experience of resource-rich countries with fiscal rules and guidelines has been mixed. Flexible fiscal guidelines seem to have worked well in some countries. The performance of rigid fiscal rules in a number of countries has been more mixed.

In some resource-rich countries, fiscal rules seem to have contributed to more prudent fiscal management and fiscal savings, at least during certain periods. Compliance with fiscal rules seems to have been better in countries that already had strong institutions and a commitment to fiscal discipline (Sharma and Strauss 2013). For example, Chile's success with its fiscal guideline (see appendix C) is seen to be mainly due to policy credibility, political commitment, and consensus—themselves the result of past prudent policies and sound institutions. In Norway, a sophisticated fiscal framework integrates a fiscal guideline and a resource fund, as discussed in box 7.1 (about Norway's fiscal guideline) and box 8.1 (about its resource fund; see chapter 8).

The design and implementation of fiscal rules have posed challenges in a number of countries, and the effects of the rules remain uncertain. To a greater or lesser extent, depending on the country, this has been primarily due to one or more of the following factors:

Box 7.1 Norway's Integrated Fiscal Framework: The Fiscal Guideline

The fiscal framework in Norway rests on two pillars: the fiscal guideline and the Government Pension Fund-Global (GPF-G), a resource fund (discussed in box 8.1, chapter 8). This framework facilitates appreciation of intertemporal challenges and provides flexibility for short-term fiscal policy aimed at macroeconomic stabilization.

The Fiscal Guideline

Fiscal policy in Norway faces long-term challenges associated with a large prospective increase in pension and health spending, and a decline in oil revenues. The fiscal guideline established in 2001 limits the central government's structural non-oil deficit over time to 4 percent (equivalent to the expected long-run real rate of return of the assets held by the GPF-G [Norway 2001]). It also indicates that fiscal policy must place emphasis on the stabilization of the economy. It allows flexibility: temporary deviations beyond the effect of the automatic non-oil stabilizers are permitted over the non-oil economic cycle.

box continues next page

Box 7.1 Norway's Integrated Fiscal Framework: The Fiscal Guideline *(continued)*

The guideline was designed to meet several policy objectives:

- *Intergenerational equity.* The 4 percent guideline preserves the value, in real terms, of the assets that have substituted oil reserves in the ground (on an expectational basis).
- *Short-run stabilization.* The guideline decouples the annual budget from oil revenue fluctuations.
- *Fighting Dutch disease.* The guideline avoids effects that would arise if oil revenues were spent immediately—which also explains why the GPF-G's assets are entirely invested abroad.

The fiscal guideline has contributed to moderating the non-oil deficit, decoupling fiscal policy from oil volatility, moderating the fluctuations of the non-oil economy, saving a large share of oil revenues, and restraining the appreciation of the currency in real terms. Several factors have contributed to its success:

- The guideline's basic elements are simple and well understood by the public.
- There has been strong consensus and commitment to the guideline.
- Flexibility makes the guideline robust, even when faced with a strong downturn—as in 2009, when, unlike fiscal rules in many other resource-rich countries, the guideline was not modified, suspended, or breached.
- The fiscal framework's credibility is supported by a very high level of fiscal transparency and strong institutions, governance, and accountability.

Source: Adapted from IMF (2009b).

- The technical difficulty of designing effective and robust rules that can withstand the uncertainty and volatility of resource revenue, rapidly changing economic environments, and structural changes in the economy.
- Complications arising from the political economy of spending resource rents, evident in the many difficulties faced by resource-rich countries seeking to secure and then maintain political consensus and commitment around a fiscal rule.
- The need to meet demanding technical and institutional prerequisites in terms of public financial management (PFM) capacity, fiscal transparency, and robust monitoring (discussed below). In particular, the performance of some fiscal rules was affected by PFM-related issues. For example, compliance with fiscal rules in Ecuador in the 2000s was complicated by the extensive revenue earmarking and budget rigidities then in place; the rules were subsequently simplified and most earmarking was eliminated in 2008 (IMF 2003; Cueva 2008; Villafuerte, López-Murphy, and Ossowski 2010). In Equatorial Guinea a non-oil golden rule was in place in the context of uncertainties regarding the proper classification of expenditures in the budget as current or capital (IMF 2005a). In Chad a system involving a rule that mandated minimum spending requirements, an oil fund, multiple budgets, revenue earmarking, and cash management fragmentation burdened administrative capacity

and hampered budget and cash management (IMF 2007b; Dabán and Hélis 2010). In recent years the focus has been on improving the overall management of the budget: for example, a new Organic Finance Law was adopted, an Integrated Financial Information Management System was implemented, the expenditure circuit was simplified and fully computerized, and other PFM reforms were introduced. In Mexico the fiscal framework included a fiscal rule together with a complex two-tier system of oil funds (Carreón-Rodríguez and Rosellón 2012; IMF 2013c). It helped insulate the non-oil budget position during budget execution, but the mechanism included rigidities, procyclicality, extrabudgetary spending, and revenue earmarking that entailed inefficiencies and complicated fiscal and asset management (Villafuerte, López-Murphy, and Ossowski 2010). Reforms to the fiscal rule and the oil funds in recent years reduced these problems to some extent.

Fiscal rules have been associated with a broad range of fiscal responses to the resource price cycle, including highly procyclical responses. For example, evidence from Latin American resource-rich countries fails to show a relationship between the presence of a fiscal rule (or a resource fund) and the degree of procyclicality of fiscal policy (Villafuerte, López-Murphy, and Ossowski 2010). In part, this is the result of the many modifications to the rules introduced in many countries, as circumstances and policy objectives changed, sometimes dramatically. Box 7.2 surveys econometric evidence on the effectiveness of fiscal rules in resource-rich countries.

Broadly speaking, rules targeting NRBs and expenditure came under pressure during the resource price boom in the 2000s, while rules targeting overall balances as well as rules targeting NRBs and expenditure were tested in the downturn in 2009–10.

During the resource boom, and under the prevailing conditions of abundant liquidity generated by rising resource revenue, a number of fiscal rules in resource-rich countries targeting the NRB and expenditure were put to the test by mounting expenditure pressures, as the increases in resource prices were increasingly seen as "permanent." A number of rules were relaxed (sometimes several times), not complied with, not implemented, or abolished. Fiscal rules targeting the overall balance achieved a greater degree of compliance. However, they provided room for expenditure increases that, while consistent with the rules, resulted in procyclical fiscal policies as resource revenue surged.

In 2009–10 some fiscal rules came under heavy pressure due to the fall in resource prices and the recession. In some countries with overall balance rules, the fall in resource revenue required large fiscal adjustments to ensure compliance, while activity was weakening. In some other countries with rules targeting the structural NRB without provisions for temporary deviations, the rules stood in the way of implementing countercyclical fiscal policies. In countries with NRB rules, such rules did not even allow nonresource automatic stabilizers to work.[4] As a result, several rules were modified or suspended.

The establishment of rigid fiscal rules would seem to be particularly problematic in postconflict resource-rich countries, resource-rich countries undergoing substantial structural change in the short and medium run, and new producers with significant future revenue uncertainties. Reform processes—such as postconflict rebuilding of the economy and institutions, state-owned enterprise (SOE) restructuring, significant reallocation of productive resources and factors of production, substantial changes in relative prices (as subsidies are reformed and price controls removed), and rapid technological change—are likely to entail major uncertainties for macroeconomic forecasts and fiscal projections, thereby complicating fiscal rule design and implementation. Significant structural change superimposed on resource revenue volatility requires ample flexibility in fiscal policy.

The experience of resource-rich countries that have adopted fiscal rules illustrates the difficulties involved in designing and implementing rules in these countries. In particular, the frequent changes to rules and compliance problems seen in many resource-rich countries highlight the challenges that the volatility and unpredictability of resource revenue pose to the design and implementation of rules and the difficult trade-offs between rigidity, flexibility, and credibility in their design. Rigid rules can easily be overcome by events, undermining their credibility, while excessive flexibility can increase uncertainty about the direction of fiscal policy.

Box 7.2 Fiscal Rules in Resource-Rich Countries: Econometric Evidence on Fiscal Impact

Empirical econometric evidence on the impact of fiscal rules on fiscal policy responses in resource-rich countries is limited:

- In a study of the fiscal responses of oil-exporting countries (OECs), Ossowski and others (2008) conclude that fiscal rules and resource funds do not have a statistically significant impact on the NRB, expenditure dynamics, or the correlation between oil revenue and expenditure.
- Arezki and Ismail (2010) find that fiscal rules in OECs have had limited success in reducing the rate of growth of current spending during booms, but may have contributed to significant reductions in capital expenditure during periods of falling oil prices.
- In a study of fiscal rules in emerging and developing economies that include but are not limited to resource-rich countries, Bova, Carcenac, and Guerguil (2014) find that having a fiscal rule does not shield these countries from procyclicality. The adoption of fiscal rules does not appear to be associated with more acyclical or countercyclical policies.
- A recent IMF study of resource-rich countries finds that fiscal rules and resource funds have not reduced the procyclicality of government expenditure in a statistically significant way (IMF 2015a; the detailed econometric analysis can be found in Bova, Medas, and Poghosyan [2016]). The study also shows the importance of institutional quality to help limit procyclicality.

Source: Authors, based on sources noted in box.

Suggestions for Fiscal Rules

The difficulties that many resource-rich countries have faced in designing and implementing successful fiscal rules suggests the need for a careful assessment of the potential benefits and costs of a fiscal rule, given country circumstances, and attention to the rule's design.

Fiscal Rule Targets

There are several types of fiscal rules, which can be distinguished by their targets. The most common are listed below.

Budget balance rules. These rules target the overall fiscal balance. They are not advisable for resource-rich countries. Although they are relatively transparent and linked to public debt objectives, overall balance rules are procyclical everywhere, and in resource-rich countries this is exacerbated by the transmission of resource revenue volatility to fiscal policy. These rules make expenditure hostage to the unpredictable fluctuations of resource revenue.

Current balance rules (also called the golden rule). These rules target the balance between current revenues and current expenditures, and are also not advisable in resource-rich countries. In addition to the problems of budget balance rules, they lack an effective fiscal anchor, since investment is not constrained. Furthermore, parts of current spending, such as health and education, represent investment in human capital. Moreover, unless PFM and fiscal accounting and transparency systems are strong, such rules could create incentives for creative accounting (the misclassification of current spending as capital spending).

Nonresource current balance rules (the nonresource golden rule) target the balance between nonresource current revenues and nonresource current expenditures. They also allow public investment to go up and down with the resource revenue flow. This instills volatility and procyclicality in capital spending and the budget, and could ignore macroeconomic absorption and institutional capacity constraints.

Structural balance (SB) rules face the challenges of estimating the structural, or long-run, price of nonrenewable resources. They are also potentially procyclical: if the estimates of the long-term resource prices are correlated with actual prices, the targeted fiscal balance is not fully decoupled from resource prices (see appendix B). In addition, the economic, institutional, and statistical preconditions for adopting SB rules are very demanding, even more so than those for other rules.

Rules that target the nonresource primary balance (NRPB) may be considered by resource-rich countries with no liquidity constraints and with sustainable fiscal positions. Focus on this indicator helps governments assess the stance and direction of fiscal policy and decouple it in the short run from the vagaries and uncertainties of resource prices and resource price forecasts. International experience suggests, however, that from a political economy point of view, these rules can come under pressure when resource prices increase on a sustained basis.

Rules that target the NRPB supplemented with additional feedback mechanisms may be considered by resource-rich countries with liquidity constraints and/ or where there are concerns regarding fiscal sustainability and vulnerability. In these cases, feedback loops from the debt or the overall balance to the fiscal rule would be incorporated to provide assurances of fiscal sustainability without losing sight of debt and financing issues.

Rules targeting the structural NRPB are an option for resource-rich countries with adequate technical capacity to produce timely and reliable estimates of the nonresource output gap (NROG), the cyclical position of the nonresource economy, and the chosen fiscal target. The structural NRPB is preferable to an overall SB. It is a better indicator of the stance and direction of fiscal policy, and of its economic effects, than the SB. It also better decouples fiscal policy from the vagaries of resource prices and forecasts. Rules targeting the structural NRPB allow for the operation of automatic stabilizers and also account for one-off or temporary factors, which are best defined early on to avoid ambiguity. On the other hand, the computation of the nonresource cycle and of automatic stabilizers is very complex and requires capacity, and could lead to unreliable results and reduced transparency.

Expenditure rules that target the nominal or real rate of increase of expenditure or its ratio to nonresource GDP share some of the characteristics of NRPB rules. By constraining the rate of increase or the level of government spending, they can provide support to efforts to limit the size of the government, should that be a policy objective. They address spending pressures directly. They are also simpler and easier to monitor and implement than NRPB or other fiscal balance rules, as only expenditure is targeted, which may be helpful in cases of severe capacity constraints. They accommodate revenue shortfalls. If nonresource revenues are very small, as in some OECs heavily dependent on oil revenues, an expenditure rule would be akin to a rule targeting the NRB or the NRPB. But expenditure rules can provide incentives for the use of tax expenditures—instead of transfers and subsidies—to achieve policy objectives. Moreover, they do not prevent tax reductions that could weaken the NRPB over time. Policy makers may try to comply with the rule by squeezing productive expenditures, including public investment. A very tight expenditure growth rule could become technically and/or politically unsustainable over time. Also, as discussed below, these rules could provide incentives to shift government expenditure off-budget, or to shift some areas of expenditure to accounting on a net basis.

Debt rules on their own are of limited use in resource-rich countries, although they could be used to supplement NRB rules. As discussed earlier, in resource-rich countries with relatively short production horizons, a wider approach to fiscal sustainability, including the depletion of resource wealth in the ground, is suggested. A partial focus on gross debt falls short of that objective. In addition, ceilings on the ratio of debt to GDP would be particularly procyclical in resource-rich countries.

If the fiscal rule targets the NRB or the NRPB, the target must take into account long-term fiscal sustainability estimates and vulnerability to resource shocks. These would be reviewed as circumstances change. However, frequent revisions to the targets—due to changes in sustainability assessments arising from movements in resource prices or resource revenue—would reintroduce procyclicality into the rule "through the back door." Hence, targets should be revised only from time to time—for example, every few years.

Rigidity versus Flexibility

Flexibility in resource-rich countries' fiscal rules is advisable. While the trade-offs between rigidity, flexibility, robustness of the rule, and credibility are complex, on balance—given the uncertainties and recurrent exogenous shocks facing resource-rich countries—fiscal rules in these countries need to incorporate ample flexibility and escape clauses. These features are necessary to enhance the robustness of the rules to unpredictable events and shocks, which in resource-rich countries are a fact of life. They help reduce the likelihood of ad hoc modifications to the rules or their outright suspension, as seen in a number of countries, which can damage the credibility of the entire fiscal framework.

Regarding flexibility, Ter-Minassian (2010) suggests various options:

- Targets can be specified for periods of a few years, with periodic revisions based on medium- and long-term reassessments.
- Temporary deviations from the targets can be allowed, with procedures for a timely return to the targets.
- Revision clauses can be introduced, specifying the conditions under which the targets may be revised.
- Rolling targets can be used—though they may weaken discipline and carry credibility costs if used inappropriately.

Fiscal guidelines with inbuilt flexibility may also be considered. Guidelines that are not legally binding and that transparently allow (i) temporary deviations from the targets, subject to specific conditions and/or (ii) well-explained changes to the targets, appear to have worked well in several countries, including Chile, Norway, and Timor-Leste.

It is important to specify escape clauses. In all cases, transparent, clear, and specific escape clauses that refer to the circumstances that would merit temporary suspension of the fiscal rule need to be put in place. This would help address unpredictable major shocks.

Finally, consensus and political commitment to the fiscal rule are vital for its success. Given the political economy issues associated with spending resource rents, these factors are perhaps even more important than in other countries.

Public Financial Management and Capacity Prerequisites

Adequate PFM capacity and fiscal transparency are key requirements for a fiscal rule, given the credibility and reputational costs associated with ambiguity or noncompliance. Ter-Minassian (2010) and Corbacho and Ter-Minassian (2013) provide comprehensive overviews of PFM preconditions for fiscal rules. They emphasize that PFM requirements for the effective implementation of fiscal rules should not be an afterthought. If PFM institutions are not up to the task, it is better to delay the introduction of fiscal rules until PFM has been upgraded. Key PFM requirements, which range across the budget process, include:

- Elaboration of annual budgets and medium-term expenditure frameworks (MTEFs) consistent with the rule, including a strong role for the ministry of finance (MoF).
- Capacity to forecast revenues and the endogenous component of expenditures, and to prepare a realistic financing plan. For example, in the case of structural rules there needs to be capacity to estimate cyclically adjusted tax bases and revenue elasticities.
- A parliamentary approval process that prevents the introduction of amendments inconsistent with the fiscal rule.
- Capacity to ensure an appropriate execution of the budget, including effective expenditure control mechanisms and the ability to introduce intrayear corrections if needed—which requires the timely availability of reliable information on budget developments.
- Comprehensive and firmly enforced accounting, budget classification, and chart of accounts systems, and reporting requirements to forestall the use of accounting tricks that would threaten and undermine the effective operation of the fiscal rule.
- Budget information mechanisms capable of generating timely and reliable statistics and reports.
- Effective independent external scrutiny, including external audit, and possibly an independent fiscal agency (see below).
- Enforcement and correction mechanisms.

An important PFM issue for fiscal rules is that they may provide incentives to resort to extrabudgetary and quasi-fiscal operations and accounting stratagems, which would undermine the integrity and credibility of the budget. Narrow coverage of the fiscal rule can be bypassed through off-budget spending. For example, in Mongolia the SB and expenditure rules established in 2010 were bypassed through large spending by the government-owned development bank, whose activities are not covered by the rule (World Bank 2014b; IMF 2014a).

Other ways to comply with fiscal rules by shifting public spending off-budget include the uncompensated provision of subsidies through SOEs; transferring public investment to SOEs; transferring spending responsibilties to subnational governments (SNGs) without making adequate financing provisions; and providing guarantees instead of explicit subsidies or transfers to enterprises and other entities. Irwin (2012) provides a thorough review of accounting devices that have been used to hide deficits or "comply" with fiscal rules.

To reduce incentives for expenditure shifting, it is important that the government provide detailed and transparent information on SOE and extrabudgetary operations and on contingent liabilities to the legislature and the public. This helps increase transparency, foster a proper evaluation of compliance with the fiscal rule in letter and in spirit, and establish accountability.

In addition to the general PFM preconditions for fiscal rules indicated above, the following preconditions are important in resource-rich countries:

- A clear fiscal accounting distinction between resource-related revenues and expenditures, and other revenues and expenditures, and the capacity to monitor them with assurances of integrity, to avoid ambiguities and prevent misclassification.
- Significant budget flexibility and limited revenue earmarking. The latter can be inconsistent with the fiscal rule to a greater degree than in other countries, because earmarking can transmit significant resource revenue volatility and procyclicality to spending (this is discussed in chapter 9).
- Fiscal transparency, including the provision of information on resource revenue developments, as well as enforcement and correction mechanisms.

The issue of capacity constraints can raise acute country-specific trade-offs for fiscal rules. Some fiscal rules may be superior in some dimensions—such as comprehensiveness of coverage or providing scope to allow automatic stabilizers to work and conduct countercyclical fiscal policies—to other rules, but are more difficult to implement. For instance, in many low-income resource-rich countries it is doubtful whether the quality and timeliness of the national accounts or available capacity at ministries of finance would support the implementation of complex SB rules that have proved challenging in some emerging and advanced economies. This would suggest consideration of simpler rules, such as expenditure rules or NRB rules, but even these rules require adequate PFM systems and fiscal transparency to forestall accounting manipulation and ensure effective implementation and integrity.

Fiscal Councils and Independent Fiscal Institutions

Fiscal councils are typically permanent executive or legislative agencies with responsibilities that mainly involve the impartial scrutiny of fiscal policies, plans, and performance (Hemming 2013b). They have usually been set up to reduce fiscal deficit biases and to help foster greater transparency (and therefore accountability) of fiscal policy.[5] This contributes to raising the political cost—in terms of the credibility of policy makers—of inappropriate uses of fiscal policy, thereby influencing the incentives that policy makers face. But fiscal councils require capacity and strong governance structures, which may be difficult to establish, especially in low-income resource exporters.

Hemming and Joyce (2013) describe the two main functions of fiscal councils as advising on fiscal policy plans (that is, reviewing and commenting on a range of fiscal policy issues) and auditing fiscal plans and performance (that is, verifying ex-ante whether the government's policies and plans will achieve their stated objectives, and ex-post whether they have been carried out as envisaged and have had their intended effects). Fiscal councils should not be confused with national audit offices, parliamentary budget and accounts committees, or other public review committees that meet periodically on fiscal matters (Hemming 2013b). In particular, the auditing functions of a fiscal council are different from those of a national audit office, which focuses on financial and performance audit. In a number of countries, fiscal councils are also directly involved in forecasting and/or program costing for the government. While the mandate of fiscal councils differs among countries, no council has been granted the power to set fiscal targets or change taxes, as this would raise serious issues of democratic accountability.

Fiscal councils can enhance transparency and accountability, provide incentives for improving fiscal management, and contribute to a more informed parliamentary and public debate through independent analysis, forecasts, and judgment. The fiscal council can provide opinions to parliament on proposed budgets, fiscal risks, MTEFs, and on long-term fiscal issues, including sustainability amid resource wealth and long-term spending pressures. It might oversee the proper transfer of resource revenue to the budget, and monitor the implementation of priority expenditure programs, with ex-post controls and assessment of government performance against expenditure composition targets and outcome indicators. These functions may be appropriate particularly in circumstances where transparency is deficient or fiscal policy is hostage to dysfunctional political processes.

Some resource-rich countries have created independent advisory committees or oversight and accountability entities, with varying degrees of success. These institutions are parallel to government oversight and audit mechanisms. Their objective is to enhance transparency, provide incentives for sound fiscal management, and strengthen public support for good resource revenue management. There is no single model, and country experience varies greatly. Box 7.3 presents five OEC examples, four of them in low-income resource-rich countries.

Box 7.3 Fiscal Councils in Resource-Rich Countries

In Mauritania, the Comité National de Suivi des Revenus des Hydrocarbures (National Committee for the Monitoring of Hydrocarbon Revenue) is composed of government officials and chaired by the treasurer. Its responsibilities are limited: it publishes monthly information on daily oil production, sales, taxes collected, and amounts placed in the petroleum fund and it estimates and monitors the transfers from the resource fund to the government (Dabán and Hélis 2010).

The Conselho Consultivo do Fundo Petrolífero (Petroleum Fund Consultative Council) in Timor-Leste is an independent watchdog made up of former government officials. It is required to comment on the annual transfer from the Petroleum Fund (a financing fund, see chapter 8) proposed in the budget. In Timor-Leste this transfer is a critical fiscal variable, as it is related to the estimated sustainable income (ESI) from oil, and it finances the non-oil deficit in its entirety. Government savings for future generations are deposited and managed in the Petroleum Fund, and the transfer therefore reduces accumulated long-term savings held in the fund. The council can also advise parliament on other matters relating to the performance and operation of the Petroleum Fund and on whether the appropriations of the Petroleum Fund are being "used effectively for the benefit of current and future generations" (Timor-Leste 2005).

In Chad, the Collège de Contrôle et de Surveillance des Revenus Pétrolièrs (Petroleum Revenue Oversight and Monitoring Committee), a joint government–civil society entity (including representatives from Parliament and the Supreme Court), was given extraordinarily wide powers. Notably, expenditure commitments and payments from the oil budget (one of four separate budgets) required the prior authorization of the collège. In practice, this ex-ante intervention in the expenditure circuit duplicated budget control mechanisms, delayed budget execution, and interfered with spending decisions. The collège also conducted ex-post assessments of oil-financed expenditures, but weak technical capacity and resources severely hampered this function (Dabán and Hélis 2010).

In São Tomé and Principe, the Comissão de Fiscalização do Petróleo (Petroleum Oversight Commission)—comprising representatives appointed by the presidency, the National Assembly, local governments, business associations, and unions—was granted wide powers of oversight of various oil accounts, as well as investigative and even judicial powers. Besides issuing reports on topics subject to its oversight, the commission could initiate investigations of irregularities; carry out searches, inspections, and seizure of documents; and judge and enforce administrative proceedings of violations of the Oil Revenue Law (São Tomé and Principe 2004).

In Mexico, the Centro de Estudios de las Finanzas Públicas (Center for the Study of Public Finances) is a parliamentary entity. Its objective is the provision of objective, impartial, and timely analytical materials on public finances and technical support to the lower chamber and parliamentary commissions. The center analyzes and assesses fiscal plans; analyzes the fiscal impact of draft laws; reviews the quarterly reports on the economic situation, public finances, and debt produced by the government; presents its own estimates and projections to congress; and reviews performance under the fiscal rule (Centro de Estudios de las Finanzas Públicas Web site).

Source: Authors, based on sources noted in box.

Some Prerequisites for Fiscal Councils in Resource-Rich Countries

An independent fiscal council is one that can openly present its analysis and conclusions without interference or fear of retribution from the executive or the legislature. Enshrining independence in legislation demonstrates political support for a fiscal council (Hemming 2013a).

The fiscal council needs to be set up with a strong governance structure and assurances of independence. The views and advice of the council can carry significant weight, and thought must be given to how to avoid it being perceived as a second audit institution or a parallel government or parliament. Steps must also be taken to forestall the risk that the council might undermine the morale of existing government institutions.

The work of a fiscal council is technically demanding, and capacity and political economy issues need to be considered (Dabán and Hélis 2010). The council must include people of strong standing and reputations who have the skills and experience in resource revenue management required to produce broad fiscal policy assessments. Their work requires adequate technical support.

Developing resource-rich countries with limited capacity would be well advised to consider carefully whether a fiscal council is warranted in the context. A fiscal council may require much scarce human capital to undertake tasks that may not be of the highest priority. Only countries with a need for the advisory and auditing input that a fiscal council can provide, and the resources to staff it without affecting government capacity, should consider them (Hemming 2013b). Those countries with limited capacity that do decide to set up fiscal councils would do well to set relatively narrow remits for them, at least in the initial stages. The design and implementation of a fiscal council needs to take into account capacity requirements and potential risks. Once sufficient capacity and credibility have been attained and progress made, the functions of the council may be gradually expanded.

Notes

1. See IMF (2009a) and Schaechter and others (2012) for background and analysis of fiscal rules, including performance in the global financial crisis. Cordes and others (2015) discuss expenditure rules. See Corbacho and Ter-Minassian (2013) for preconditions for introducing fiscal rules, and Ter-Minassian (2010) for preconditions for structural fiscal rules.

2. The lists provide examples of countries that have targeted certain fiscal indicators, either in the past or currently. The inclusion of a country in a certain category does not necessarily imply that the fiscal rule is currently in place—the rule may have been in place in the past and subsequently been changed or eliminated.

3. Supranational fiscal rules apply to members of the Central African Economic and Monetary Community (CEMAC), of which Cameroon, Chad, the Republic of Congo, Gabon, and Equatorial Guinea are oil-exporting countries (OECs). The CEMAC supranational fiscal rules target the central government basic balance, defined as the difference between total revenue excluding grants and total expenditure excluding

foreign-financed investment, and the public debt ratio. In 2008 the CEMAC Commission introduced two supplementary criteria: the basic structural fiscal balance (derived from the basic balance by replacing actual oil revenue with its three-year moving average), and the basic non-oil balance (as a share of non-oil gross domestic product—GDP). Countries' compliance with the supranational fiscal rules has been mixed.

4. Automatic stabilizers are the fiscal revenue and expenditure items that adjust automatically to cyclical changes in the economy. For example, as output falls in a recession, revenue collections will decline, while expenditure on unemployment benefits will increase as jobs are lost. Hence, in a recession and in the absence of discretionary fiscal policy measures, the fiscal position is typically expected to deteriorate (Baunsgaard and Symansky 2009).

5. See Kumar and Ter-Minassian (2007) and, specifically for resource-rich countries, Dabán and Hélis (2010).

CHAPTER 8

Resource Funds

Many resource-rich countries have established resource funds in response to the challenges and complications that resource revenue poses to fiscal policy and asset management. In some of these countries, the fund is part of a fiscal framework that includes a fiscal rule or guideline.[1]

Resource funds form part of a wider set of funds known as sovereign wealth funds (SWFs). SWFs make up a heterogeneous group of funds, with various objectives, asset accumulation and withdrawal mechanisms, and institutional features (see Das, Mazarei, and van der Hoorn 2010).

What objectives do governments of resource-rich countries pursue when establishing a resource fund? These funds have been set up for different purposes. In many cases, governments that created resource funds pursued more than one objective. The following main objectives can be discerned:

Fiscal and macroeconomic stabilization. As discussed above, highly volatile and uncertain resource revenues can have a negative impact on macroeconomic and financial stability. The objective of *stabilization funds* is to help governments manage budget volatility and uncertainty.

Savings. Oil and mineral resources are exhaustible and run the risk of obsolescence. *Savings funds* aim to turn at least part of a country's resource wealth into other forms of wealth—to create a store of wealth that will allow future generations to benefit from revenues generated by the depletion of current resources.

Budget financing: stabilization and saving. A few funds are aligned with fiscal balances: they receive budget surpluses, and finance budget deficits. These *financing funds* thus have both stabilization and savings objectives.

National development and portfolio management. This includes several cases. Some resource-rich countries have created resource funds as separate entities with authority to undertake domestic investment or otherwise spend off budget for *public policy* purposes; many recent funds have national development as an objective, which may be combined with stabilization and/or savings aims. Some governments have allowed their funds to invest in domestic financial assets (DFAs) purely on *commercial* grounds, as part of their portfolio management strategies, or with *dual commercial/policy* objectives.

Stabilization Funds, Savings Funds, and Financing Funds

It is important to clarify the difference between resource funds with stabilization or savings objectives, and fiscal rules. Resource funds do not place formal restrictions on fiscal policy, as fiscal rules do. Rather, these funds are expected to improve fiscal management and influence fiscal policy indirectly.

How are stabilization or savings objectives translated into resource fund operational rules for the accumulation and withdrawal of resources? In other words, how do these funds work? Again, the *operational* rules of a fund should not be be confused with *fiscal* rules. The discussion that follows is about the operational accumulation and withdrawal rules of resource funds. Stabilization funds, savings funds, and financing funds will be discussed in turn.

Stabilization funds aim to reduce the short-term impact of volatile resource revenue on the budget and the economy, and to support fiscal discipline. Most of these funds have rigid price- or revenue-contingent deposit and withdrawal operational rules. Deposits and withdrawals depend on the realization of an outcome (resource price or revenue) relative to a specified trigger. In some cases, the entire "excess revenue" relative to the revenue computed at the level of the benchmark trigger is mandated to be deposited in the fund; in others, this is only a specified share—and the same applies to permissible withdrawals. In some funds, limits are placed on the total accumulation of fund assets.

The operational objective of stabilization funds is to reduce the volatility and uncertainty of resource revenue flows to the budget. Reduced revenue volatility would, in turn, facilitate the decoupling of budget expenditure from changes in revenue flows and save resources that can be used later when prices fall. When resource prices are "high," the expectation is that making deposits in the fund—and therefore making those resources unavailable to the budget—will help "discipline the budget" and contain spending. When prices are "low," the fund is expected to act as a damper or buffer (through the transfer of funds to the budget) to forestall unpredictable fiscal adjustments.

If the fund is to function as a stabilization mechanism and financial buffer, its assets cannot be held domestically. If the fund were to invest domestically during a boom or to liquidate domestic assets during a slump, this would exacerbate macroeconomic volatility.

Stabilization funds do not reduce the revenue volatility and uncertainty faced by the public sector as a whole. The reduction of volatility and uncertainty of budget revenue is achieved by transferring volatility and uncertainty to the fund.

Two types of contingent mechanisms for the accumulation and withdrawal of assets are most frequently used:[2]

- Rules contingent on resource prices or revenues that are prespecified in advance (either fixed or set through a formula). Examples of current or earlier resource funds with these rules include Chile (copper stabilization fund until 2006), the Russian Federation, Sudan, and República Bolivariana de Venezuela.
- Rules contingent on the difference between the price (revenue) set in the budget for the current year—which can be specified on an ad hoc basis or by formula—and the actual price (revenue). Examples include Alberta (since 2004), Algeria, Bahrain, Ghana, the Islamic Republic of Iran (until 2010), Libya, Mexico, Mongolia, Oman (since 1998), Qatar, and Trinidad and Tobago.

Certain accumulation rules for stabilization funds may turn them partly into savings funds. If the accumulation rule is set conservatively as a matter of strategy (that is, with "low" price or revenue triggers for deposits into the fund), stabilization funds in fact also fulfil a "savings" role on an expectational basis, at least in terms of there being a significant probability of holding a growing amount of gross financial assets (as in Trinidad and Tobago in recent years).

Savings funds aim to create a store of wealth for future generations. They typically have rigid noncontingent operational rules. The rules require the deposit of a specified share of resource revenue, or of total revenues, into the fund. For example, the Kuwaiti Reserve Fund for Future Generations required the deposit of 10 percent of total budget revenue; this was raised to 25 percent in 2013. Rules for the withdrawal of resources from these funds vary, and in some cases are not clearly specified. The scope for withdrawals from the fund to finance the budget adds a stabilization element beyond the main savings objective.

Examples of current or earlier savings funds include those in the U.S. state of Alaska, the Canadian province of Alberta (until 1987), Angola, Azerbaijan, Chad (fund eliminated in 2005), Ecuador (fund eliminated in 2008), Equatorial Guinea, Gabon, the Islamic Republic of Iran (since 2010), Kazakhstan, Kuwait, Mauritania, Oman (until 1998), Russia (since 2008, together with another fund), and São Tomé and Principe.

Financing funds, in contrast to the funds discussed above, have flexible operational mechanisms aligned with overall fiscal balances. Their operational objective is to finance the budget: the fund accumulates budget surpluses and finances budget deficits. Operationally, the fund receives all resource revenue, and finances the budget's nonresource deficit by way of a reverse transfer.

Therefore, unlike the funds discussed above, these funds do not try to "discipline" expenditure through the removal of resources from the budget. The flows in and out of the fund depend on resource revenue, and on macroeconomic conditions and policy decisions embodied in the nonresource fiscal stance. Moreover, unlike some stabilization and savings funds (SSFs), these funds have no spending authority: all expenditure is on budget. They also provide an explicit and transparent link between fiscal policy and asset accumulation and address fungibility issues, because the mechanism rules out financing the accumulation of assets in the fund through borrowing or running down other assets.

Only a handful of resource-rich countries have financing funds: Chile, Norway, and Timor-Leste. Interestingly, they encompass a broad range of levels of development. Box 8.1 discusses the Norwegian financing fund.

Box 8.1 Norway's Integrated Fiscal Framework: The Government Pension Fund

The government established the State Petroleum Fund in 1990. The fund was renamed Government Pension Fund-Global (GPF-G) in 2006. The change in the fund's name was made solely to emphasize the rapid increase in pension expenditure expected in future years. The fund's resources are not earmarked to pensions or to any other component of expenditure. The fund was not activated until 1995, when the overall fiscal position switched to surplus: under the fund's mechanism, net transfers are only made to the fund if there is a central government surplus.

The GPF-G is a financing fund aimed at fostering fiscal transparency. The preparatory work that led to its creation emphasized that the fund must be incorporated within a coherent budgetary process. The fund receives net oil revenues and makes a transfer to the budget to finance the non-oil deficit. The accumulation of assets in the fund reflects surpluses. This design forestalls transfers to the fund financed by borrowing. It also avoids asset and liability management problems that affect funds with rigid rules, discussed below.

The fund cannot spend or invest domestically. It can only invest in external assets. This avoids a dual budget and preserves the integrity of the nation's budget. All fiscal policy and expenditure decisions are taken in the budget, in the broad context provided by the fiscal guideline (see box 7.1, chapter 7).

Norway's ministry of finance (MoF) has the responsibility of managing the GPF-G. It has delegated the operational management to Norges Bank (the central bank) on the basis of regulations, guidelines, and a management agreement, all of which are public information. The asset management objective is to maximize returns subject to compliance with the investment guidelines. Any major proposed changes to the investment strategy are presented to parliament to ensure political support for strategic decisions of importance to future generations.

The GPF-G has no separate legal status and does not have a board. It is formally an account kept by the MoF at Norges Bank, which invests the value of the account in international financial markets in its own name, via the bank's own assets management division—Norges Bank Investment Management (NBIM).

The fund is supported by strong levels of transparency and governance, which together with assurances of integrity and the provision of public information, buttress the fund's credibility. Transparency is a key factor in the political economy of the fund. As Skancke (2003) noted, if there is a need to build consensus around saving the equivalent of 100 percent of gross domestic product (GDP) or more in financial assets, policy makers must be willing to tell the public exactly how they are going to invest those resources and what the returns on the investments are.

Source: Adapted from IMF (2009b, 2014b).

The implementation of SSFs with rigid rules has often been based at least in part on political economy considerations. It is often expected that the removal of "high" resource revenue relative to some benchmark, or of a share of such revenue from the budget, will stabilize and/or moderate public expenditure, thereby reducing discretion in fiscal policy, and encourage savings. It is important to note, however, that resource funds do not affect public spending directly, except in very specific circumstances. The technical and political economy aspects of this issue are often confused and it is useful to clarify them, as follows.

- At a *technical level*, if there are strong liquidity constraints, and if the fund rules are binding and they are observed, the requirement to place assets in the fund will force spending reductions or tax increases compared to the alternative situation without a fund. But if the government is running surpluses, removing some resources from the budget does not necessarily entail a need for reductions in expenditure, even if there are liquidity constraints.
- In the absence of liquidity constraints, even if the government is not running a surplus, it can borrow or run down other financial assets to increase spending and make the required deposits in the fund. Sometimes it is thought that money that has to be parked away in a fund is "safeguarded" from improper use, and saved. But this is not necessarily the case, because borrowing can take place at the same time and money is fungible.[3] The advantage of putting money into a fund—according to some rule unrelated to optimal risk and liquidity management—while borrowing at the same time, and often at a higher cost is not clear. Alternatively, the government may simply decide to ignore the fund rules.
- This would still leave open possible *political economy* arguments for rigid fund rules: even if the government is running a surplus or there are no liquidity constraints, rules that mandate deposits into a fund can influence the political process in the direction of moderating spending. The evidence suggests, however, that the political economy advantages of removing resources from the budget are often unclear; that when pressures are brought to bear, the funds' rules can be changed, bypassed, temporarily suspended, or ignored; and that the results seem to be very country specific.

Therefore, since money is fungible, the effectiveness of rigid resource fund rules for stabilization and saving is in principle uncertain. On the other hand, rigid fund rules can have fiscal costs in terms of suboptimal asset and liability management.

Tensions can arise between funds with rigid rules, fiscal policy, and asset and liability management, and this can lead to inefficiencies. That is likely to happen especially in situations of significant exogenous shocks; changes in policy priorities; mounting spending pressures; and conflicting objectives between the fund, fiscal policy, and asset management.

The rules may not be appropriate for the specific circumstances. They may create dilemmas for policy makers. For example, the fund's accumulation rules may require that deposits be made to the fund; but if the budget is in deficit, the government has to borrow or run down other assets, or cut spending, or increase taxes to make the deposits, which may not be the best course of action. Accumulating assets in a resource fund to comply with fund rule requirements and adding to the public debt at the same time is a costly strategy, especially if the spread between the rates of return on fund assets and the cost of government borrowing is significant.

Finally, resource funds with rigid operational rules in conjunction with fiscal rules can make the fiscal framework overdetermined and compound policy dilemmas. The fiscal rules and the fund's operational rules may be mutually inconsistent in certain circumstances, leading to the need for difficult choices between compliance and avoiding inefficiency and fiscal costs. More important, the rationale for a resource fund with rigid operational rules when there is a fiscal rule is unclear. What would the fund add to the fiscal rule? Perhaps there are doubts that the fiscal rule alone is adequate to ensure fiscal discipline? Moreover, if the fund is set up with mainly asset management objectives, those would not be helped by rigid accumulation and withdrawal rules. Thus, if a fiscal rule or guideline is in place and there is a desire for a resource fund, the best option is likely to be a financing fund with flexible accumulation and withdrawal principles, as in Chile, Norway, and Timor-Leste.

Stabilization, Savings, and Financing Funds: International Experience

Evidence from a number of countries shows that it has been difficult to set trigger resource prices or revenues in contingent stabilization funds. This is mainly due to the nature of the stochastic process that generates those prices. It is very difficult to set average long-term prices as triggers with any degree of confidence, or to determine early on whether a given price shock is transitory or long-lasting. A shock that turns out to be long-lasting could lead to the unsustainability of the fund. Resource price volatility and shock persistence also imply that long, backward-looking, moving average formulas to set triggers are likely to deviate markedly and during long periods from actual prices, testing the liquidity and robustness of the fund to changing environments.

In some cases, governments complied with fund rules that turned out to be ill-suited to the particular circumstances, at the cost of inefficiencies and suboptimal results. Often, however, when significant conflicts among policy objectives arose, rigid rules were modified, suspended, or ignored—or, in some cases, the fund was eliminated.

A number of stabilization funds have undergone changes, sometimes frequent, in the trigger prices or in the revenue base for the calculation of deposits, often due to tensions that arose between fund rules and fiscal policy. Changes to the rules have often been made in response to changes in international prices, expenditure pressures, or shifting policy priorities (as in Algeria, Kazakhstan, República

Bolivariana de Venezuela, and Russia). In some cases the fund's assets ran out (for example, Mexico's Stabilization Fund in 2002).

Savings funds have also had changes in their operational rules. In the 1980s and 1990s the rules of funds in Alaska, the United States; of Alberta, Canada; Oman; and Papua New Guinea (among others) were changed—in some cases several times—to accommodate exogenous changes or expenditure pressures. In more recent times, the rules of other funds were also changed.

In view of the inconsistencies that arose between fund rules and other policy objectives given changing circumstances, some countries opted to not comply with the deposit rules or to temporarily suspend their application (examples include Alberta, Canada; Gabon; the Islamic Republic of Iran; Sudan; and República Bolivariana de Venezuela). Some others abolished their funds (Chad in 2005, Ecuador in 2008, Nigeria in the 1990s, and Papua New Guinea in 1999).

Specific country experience can illustrate these issues in more detail:

- República Bolivariana de Venezuela was only able to deposit the resources required by its stabilization fund rule in certain years in the early 2000s, by issuing debt at higher interest rates than the returns on the fund's assets, given the overall stance of fiscal policies. This led to frequent changes in fund rules and temporary suspensions of the operations of the fund (Financial Times 2000; Davis and others 2003; Manzano and others 2012).
- In some years during the 2000s, Algeria and Ecuador made deposits into their funds while issuing debt that was serviced by the fund itself (IMF 2005b; Ossowski and others 2008; Villafuerte, López-Murphy, and Ossowski 2010).
- Gabon sometimes made deposits into its savings fund with low returns, while at the same time paying significantly higher interest rates on its high public external debt and incurring debt service arrears (IMF 2004, 2005c).
- In Chad and Ecuador in the 2000s, in contexts of extensive revenue earmarking and fragmentation of cash-flow management, compliance with fund deposit rules took place at times while the central government was experiencing liquidity problems and payment arrears were being incurred at the same time (IMF 2006a; Dabán and Hélis 2010). Both funds were eliminated, as noted above.
- In Alaska (the United States) deposits were sometimes made into the fund, and dividends paid from the fund to the population (which over time came to be considered as entitlements), while the state general fund operated at a substantial deficit (Goldsmith 2004). Appendix D provides a discussion of the issues surrounding the direct distribution of revenues to the population.

Stabilization funds with rigid rules aimed at stabilizing budget revenue during the fiscal year have been more resilient, but some new funds with formula-based trigger prices have faced difficulties (see below). These funds can also provide incentives for the strategic setting of the resource price or revenue in the budget if those are not set by formula. Setting a "high" price in the budget raises the probability that resources can be withdrawn from the fund during budget execution. More broadly, expenditure can still be increased during the year even if the required transfers are made to the fund. Finally, if annual budget expenditures are prudently determined within a medium-term expenditure framework (MTEF), and there are reasonable liquidity cushions that can be used flexibly in case of downturns (as suggested above), then it is redundant to have an arbitrary and mechanistic arrangement that shifts money away from the budget when resource revenue is higher than budgeted, or provides money to the budget when it is lower.

The adoption of rigid rules in some new funds has posed problems of coordination between fund operations on the one hand, and fiscal policy and asset management on the other, after only a few years of fund operations. Or the funds might face potential difficulties in light of recent medium-term projections regarding the countries' public finances. In all these cases, complications have resulted, or are likely to result, from operational requirements that deposits must be made in the fund, without regard to the overall fiscal position (box 8.2).

Box 8.2 Early Signs of Stress or Potential Stress in New Resource Funds with Rigid Rules

Ghana. As oil revenues started to flow, the Petroleum Revenue Management Act (PRMA) of 2011 established a system of oil revenue allocations, oil funds, and earmarking. All oil revenues would be received by a Petroleum Holding Fund, which would then disburse them according to formulas to the budget and to two oil funds—the Stabilization Fund and the Heritage Fund. A "petroleum benchmark revenue" was defined on the basis of moving average formulas comprising past, current, and expected future values. The budget received an annual budget funding amount (ABFA) from oil revenue that could not exceed 70 percent of the petroleum benchmark revenue. In addition, 70 percent of the ABFA was earmarked to public investment. The two oil funds would receive all revenues in excess of the ABFA, according to specified shares (Ghana 2011).

This framework raised some operational issues in implementation. In 2013–14 the framework required the authorities to transfer resources to the funds while the central government was running large deficits and public debt was rising steeply. In 2013 the transfer to the funds was higher than the ABFA at a time when the government's deficit was on the order of 10 percent of gross domestic product (GDP) (see Ghana 2013, 2014; IMF 2015c). After two-and-a-half years of implementation of the PRMA, the ministry of finance (MoF) indicated to parliament that it (and other stakeholders) had identified inconsistencies and operational and administrative challenges of the system that, in their view, needed to be addressed (Ghana 2013). In 2014 the resources in the Stabilization Fund were capped (as allowed under the PRMA), and excess balances were transferred to a contingency fund

box continues next page

and for debt repayment (Ghana 2014). The PRMA was recently amended; under one of the amendments, the MoF can propose a revision of the benchmark petroleum revenue to parliament in case of unexpected changes in petroleum prices or output. Another amendment sets a minimum transfer to the funds of 30 percent of the petroleum benchmark revenue (Ghana 2015).

Mongolia. A Stabilization and Savings Fund (SSF) with contingent rules was established as part of the Fiscal Stability Law (FSL) enacted in 2010 to manage rapidly growing mining revenues and improve fiscal stability and discipline. The FSL set up three fiscal rules and the fund. The fiscal rules comprise ceilings on the structural budget deficit, expenditure growth, and public debt. The structural deficit is here defined as the difference between structural revenues and spending, where mineral structural revenues are defined as a 16-year backward and forward moving average of past mineral prices and futures prices (actual prices of the last 12 years and futures prices for the current year and the next 3 years). The rules became effective in 2013, and can be recalibrated every 4 years.

The SSF receives transfers from the budget when actual mining revenues exceed structural revenues as defined above. The difference between the two is allocated to the fund. This requirement applies even if there is an overall fiscal deficit (IMF 2014a). In 2011–12 transfers to the fund amounting to a cumulative 2¼ percent of GDP had to be made because mining revenues exceeded structural revenues, while the general government ran deficits of 4 percent of GDP in 2011 and 9 percent in 2012 (derived from IMF 2015d). The transfers were financed from government borrowing, and no net financial wealth was accumulated.

The Islamic Republic of ***Iran.*** The National Development Fund of Iran (NDFI) was established in 2010 to promote national development and diversification, and savings. The fund lends to the private sector. The fund's revenues consist of a specific and rising share of oil and gas export revenues, irrespective of oil, macroeconomic, or fiscal developments.

The mechanism for allocating resources to the NDFI is too rigid and detached from macroeconomic and fiscal conditions. In recent years, the fund accumulated significant resources at a time when the budget was facing a severe fiscal revenue shortfall. Given liquidity constraints, the government was forced to cut government expenditure significantly (including deep cuts in public investment) and resort to monetary financing, while resources mounted in the NDFI (IMF 2014c, 2014d).

Angola. The Fundo Soberano de Angola (FSDEA) was set up in 2012 with three objectives: capital preservation, maximization of long-term returns, and domestic infrastructure development. The fund received an initial endowment and will receive an annual transfer, equivalent to a specified volume of oil at current oil prices, regardless of the overall fiscal position. In addition, oil revenue arising from higher actual oil prices than budgeted must be transferred to a treasury deposit account.

box continues next page

Box 8.2 Early Signs of Stress or Potential Stress in New Resource Funds with Rigid Rules *(continued)*

The International Monetary Fund (IMF) has projected persistent and relatively large fiscal deficits over the medium term, leading to increasing gross financing needs and rising public debt ratios, while at the same time accumulating assets at the FSDEA, and possibly the treasury reserve account (IMF 2014e, 2014f, 2014g).

Gabon. In 2012 the existing Fonds pour les Générations Futures was renamed the Fonds Souverain de la République Gabonaise (FSRG), and an agency was created to identify long-term investments for the FSRG, which would be a savings fund with investments in Gabon. Until the fund's capital reaches a preestablished minimum level, the fund will receive 10 percent of annual budgeted oil revenues, 50 percent of the difference (if any) between actual total budget revenues and the revenue projection in the budget, and dividends from public investments and state participation. Once the minimum capital level is reached, the FSRG will receive 25 percent of the income on its investments, and the difference between actual and budgeted oil revenues (Gabon 2012; IMF 2013b). The IMF, however, has projected low fiscal deficits or a broad fiscal balance over the next few years (IMF 2013b, 2015e).

Source: Authors, based on sources noted in box.

Financing funds with flexible rules have avoided the problems just discussed. In the countries that have these funds, fiscal policy and savings objectives have been set directly in fiscal guidelines, and the fund is merely a financing mechanism for the budget.

Effectiveness of Stabilization, Savings, and Financing Funds

The evidence on the effectiveness of resource funds with stabilization and savings objectives is mixed. Countries with financing funds and flexible fiscal guidelines have generally been praised for their macroeconomic and public wealth management. In many other countries, however, the existence of a resource fund (even in countries that also have fiscal rules) does not appear to have had a positive impact on macroeconomic and fiscal outcomes, nor on government saving. There is little evidence of a dampening effect of resource funds on policy procyclicality. Accumulation of gross assets in a resource fund has not necessarily represented genuine financial saving and wealth accumulation (Heuty and Aristi 2010; Villafuerte, López-Murphy, and Ossowski 2010; Natural Resource Governance Institute 2014; Bova, Medas, and Poghosyan 2016). The econometric evidence is reviewed in box 8.3.

Domestic Operations of Resource Funds

A number of resource funds, including many of recent vintage, are allowed to undertake domestic operations. For example, certain funds in Algeria, Angola,

---

Box 8.3 Resource Funds: Econometric Evidence on Fiscal and Macroeconomic Impact

Econometric evidence on the impact of resource funds is limited, and mixed:

- Clemente, Faris, and Puente (2002) analyze the performance of the Macroeconomic Stabilization Investment Fund in República Bolivariana de Venezuela. Using a general equilibrium model, the authors conclude that the fund increased the volatility of macroeconomic variables.
- The evidence in a study of nonrenewable resource funds by Crain and Devlin (2003) provides little support for the ability of funds to reduce fiscal volatility.
- Shabsigh and Ilahi (2007) conclude that the presence of a resource fund in oil-exporting countries (OECs) contributes toward reducing domestic inflation, the real exchange rate, and price and money volatility.
- As noted earlier, Ossowski and others (2008) find that funds do not have a statistically significant impact on key fiscal variables.
- An analysis of the correlation between the presence of fiscal rules and/or funds in OECs, and the degree of fiscal policy procyclicality during the recent oil price cycle—based on the data in Villafuerte and López-Murphy (2010)—does not show statistically significant differences in the fiscal policy responses of countries with these mechanisms and those without them.
- Sugawara (2014), on the other hand, finds that government expenditure is less volatile in resource-rich countries with stabilization funds than in those without.
- A recent International Monetary Fund study (cited in box 7.2) finds that resource funds have not reduced the procyclicality of government spending in a statistically significant way (IMF 2015a; Bova, Medas, and Poghosyan 2016).

Source: Authors, based on sources noted in box.

Azerbaijan, Gabon, the Islamic Republic of Iran, Kuwait, Qatar, Russia, and the United Arab Emirates have invested abroad and also carry out operations at home. In addition, several countries have established or are in the process of establishing sovereign development funds that invest only domestically—the strategic investment funds (SIFs).

The use of resource funds for domestic investment has become increasingly popular in recent years, predominantly in emerging markets and developing economies. This is likely to have been at least partly related to abundant inflows of resource-related revenues during the commodity boom that led to public spending increases and creation of funds in a number of countries, exceptionally low yields on foreign assets that lowered the perceived opportunity cost of domestic investment (including financial investment), and political economy considerations.

Should resource funds undertake domestic investment and spending? It is necessary to distinguish different cases according to the objectives and the financial and economic rigor of investment criteria. First, funds that invest or spend domestically only for *public policy purposes*. These funds do not require a defined commercial rate of return on their investments, and their spending could be implemented through the budget. Second, funds that have a "double bottom line" investment criterion of a *commercial financial return and an economic impact*. And third, funds that hold domestic financial assets (DFAs) purely on a *commercial basis* as part of their portfolio management. These cases will be discussed in turn.

Funds that Undertake Public Investment and Current Spending for Public Policy Purposes

Domestic investment and other spending undertaken by resource funds only for public policy purposes are noncommercial activities that could be replicated through the government budget's tax and expenditure policies. For example, the public investment carried out by a fund could, under an alternative setup, be on budget. Social transfers from the fund also could be executed by the budget. The various reasons put forth for establishing this type of a fund include:

- To get around weak public financial management (PFM) systems and an ineffective, inefficient, or corrupt budget system; and to deliver through a fund with separate procedures and control systems expenditure of better quality and at a lower cost (the "islands of excellence" argument).
- To prevent potential overspending or rent capture by keeping resources off-budget and managed by a separate entity.
- To support development by undertaking public investment projects in infrastructure or social infrastructure, delivering public services, or financing the private sector based on public policy objectives. Sometimes these fund activities may be motivated, at least in part, by political economy considerations— that is, by showing that the resource revenue is being put to good use.

There are various ways a fund can spend or encumber resources for public policy purposes:

- Spend directly off-budget.
- Provide off-budget subsidies or domestic loans to public enterprises or the private sector, undertake equity investment in private domestic companies, or participate in special purpose vehicles (SPVs) cofinanced by the private sector (for example, for infrastructure projects) for noncommercial public policy purposes.
- Provide guarantees to SPVs, public enterprises, or private companies, generating contingent liabilities.

Resource fund spending for this category of funds raises some fundamental macroeconomic and PFM questions:

- Investing or spending domestically could transmit resource revenue volatility to the economy and be procyclical. What will ensure that resource fund expenditures do not undermine macroeconomic stability or contribute to Dutch disease?
- How will fund spending be protected from revenue volatility?
- How will overall spending priorities be set? Which expenditures will be financed by the budget and which by the fund, and why? How will coordination with the budget be ensured to prevent fiscal fragmentation and dual budget problems? How will the standing of the standard budget as the main fiscal management tool be preserved?
- Will fund investment pass the tests of appraisal, contestability, and prioritization?
- What expenditure commitment and procurement systems will be used?
- Will the expenditures by the fund be subject to adequate control, accounting, reporting, audit, ex-post evaluation, and disclosure mechanisms?
- How will fund performance be assessed and managerial accountability maintained if fund managers can claim that domestic public investment requirements stand in the way of achieving satisfactory rates of return on fund assets?
- How will political capture of the fund by special interests be forestalled, and governance concerns addressed?

In practice, the evidence does not support claims that noncommercial public investment by resource funds is superior to budget spending and that the "islands of excellence" argument holds in resource-rich countries. Indeed, in a number of cases, lack of transparency in fund expenditure and other operations has hampered legitimacy, and over time undermined public support for the fiscal policy objectives related to the fund's operations.

A number of funds have been the subject of pressures to capture their expenditures, finance politically motivated projects, and increase government spending outside the budget. In some cases, the limited expertise of resource funds with public service delivery, and limited accountability, have raised serious concerns about the effectiveness, prioritization, and probity of such spending (Shields 2013). Furthermore, the use of funds to bypass the budget can have a negative impact on the development of the PFM system: scarce resources are diverted to the fund, and there may be less scrutiny of the core budget. Box 8.4 provides some examples.

It is sometimes argued that it makes little sense for the funds of developing resource-rich countries to place assets abroad, because the marginal productivity of domestic public capital is higher than the yield on foreign assets: the funds should foster development by undertaking domestic investment. These arguments arise from a partial and fragmented view of public finance and a misunderstanding of the role of the fund. Decisions on the allocation of revenue for investment at home or abroad are independent of whether a resource fund is in place. The existence of a fund—an *institutional* issue—is irrelevant for the strate-

Box 8.4 Resource Funds and Extrabudgetary Spending

In Nigeria in the 1990s off-budget funds financed by oil revenues undertook large extrabudgetary spending that was nontransparent and reflected a lack of budget control. Extrabudgetary spending was financed from oil revenues kept outside the Federation Account and
sometimes from stabilization accounts. The expenditures were not covered by the warrants
system, and therefore their nature was not well known; a large share of the resources was
directed toward supporting nonperforming state-owned enterprises (SOEs). As oil-financed
extrabudgetary expenditures grew strongly, reaching 53 percent of nondebt expenditure in
1993, the formal budget lost much of its meaning (Moser, Rogers, and van Til 1997). In the
end, the funds were abolished. Nigeria has recently set up a new fund, the Nigeria Sovereign
Investment Authority, which aims to operate to a greater extent on commercial terms, also
with regard to domestic investments.

The Venezuelan Investment Fund (FIV) was set up to act as the repository of the oil
windfall in the 1970s. It received significant off-budget resources. However, instead of
sterilizing the windfall, its resources were soon diverted toward equity participation in
public enterprises (including energy-intensive industries, many of which turned out to
be loss makers and a source of recurrent expenditure for the government) and
to provide cash injections to the electricity sector to help finance its losses (Manzano
and others 2012).

In its initial period, Alberta's Heritage Savings Trust Fund (AHSTF) provided low-interest
financing to state firms, undertook off-budget economic development and social investments, and granted loans to priority sectors. The poor results achieved—the funding of
uneconomic projects resulted in the need to write off many loans—led to a radical overhaul
of the fund in 1997. Notably, it was decided that the AHSTF would no longer be used for
economic development or social investment purposes (Warrack and Keddie, undated;
Smith 1991).

The Oil Stabilization Fund in the Islamic Republic of Iran was set up to act as a fiscal stabilization mechanism, but it also set aside 50 percent of its capital to provide lending in foreign
currency at subsidized interest rates to domestic private sector activities—deemed to be
priorities in the Islamic Republic of Iran's official Five-Year Development Plans. According to
Amuzegar (2005), the operations of the fund lacked transparency and there was little information on investment performance. The fund's board was often bypassed by other sectors
of government that required the fund to finance various projects, not always consistent with
its objectives. Although the budget law precluded the use of fund resources for the financing of budget deficits unless oil revenue fell short of the budgeted amount, this objective
was sometimes bypassed through off-budget appropriations out of the fund. Arguably, an
institution set up to help stabilize the economy became at times a destabilizing factor. Currently, the fund is de facto not operational, and a new fund, the National Development Fund
of Iran (NDFI), was set up in 2010 (see box 8.2).

Source: Authors, based on sources noted in box.

gic *policy* issue of how to allocate scarce public resources. If public noncommercial domestic investment is a better use of public resources than foreign asset accumulation once all the multiple dimensions of this issue have been evaluated, then the investment should be undertaken, preferably by the budget (for the reasons discussed above), and the resource fund would simply receive less resources to place abroad.

Finally, the assignment of public spending or public investment responsibilities to the resource fund can lead to confusion about potentially competing fund objectives, and complications in ex-post assessments of fund performance. Fund managers need to report on fund performance, primarily on financial returns. An emphasis on, or a requirement to undertake, domestic spending or investment for public policy purposes may stand in the way of achieving an acceptable risk-adjusted rate of return on the fund's assets or holding an adequate level of precautionary liquid assets. It can also hamper accountability, because fund managements can claim that financial results are due in part to policy-oriented noncommercial requirements imposed on them.

In light of the discussion above, it is not recommended that the resource fund undertake noncommercial public policy expenditures. These need to be kept on budget. The fund's purpose requires focusing on the maximization of financial returns subject to tolerable risk and desired liquidity restrictions. This then raises the issue of whether the fund's mandate may include the authority to undertake domestic *financial* investment *as part of its asset management*. This is discussed next.

Investment in Domestic Financial Assets for Commercial or Near-Commercial Purposes

Some SWFs, including a number of resource funds, invest in DFAs. Several SWFs (including pension reserve funds such as New Zealand's Superannuation Fund) hold significant DFAs in their portfolios. Others, for example those in Malaysia and Singapore, started as state-holding companies tasked with improving the competitiveness of public enterprises and moving some of them toward partial or full public offerings; these funds later diversified into foreign and DFAs.

As indicated above, resource funds may invest in DFAs either on purely commercial grounds, as part of their asset management strategies, or also with other objectives such as supporting private sector development, financing infrastructure by acting as a cornerstone investor in public-private partnership (PPP) projects, deepening undercapitalized domestic capital markets, and attracting foreign investment to strategic sectors, as in the case of SIFs (see Halland, Noel, and Tordo [forthcoming 2016] for an overview of SIFs).

The use of SWFs for domestic financial investment has been the subject of much debate.

On the one hand, it is argued that the resources of capital-scarce countries could reap higher risk-adjusted returns from investing commercially at home than by investing in global financial markets, potentially with important positive externalities. Funds with knowledge of local markets and long-term investment horizons could be used for commercial or near-commercial domestic investment, including strategic investment in sectors that are seen as economically important and that at the same time yield commercially competitive risk-adjusted returns on financial investment. Some domestically focused funds have been able to achieve returns well above the market (Clark and Monk 2015).

On the other hand, there are concerns over the potential quality of the investments and the returns on DFAs. In particular, the owner of the fund—the government—may be the same entity promoting the financial investments, potentially generating conflicts of interest. There may also be risks of political capture, poor investment decisions, and governance issues, as well as procyclicality and greater macroeconomic volatility (Gelb, Tordo, and Halland 2014).

The differences between resource funds and nonresource SWFs, SIFs, and other publicly owned investment funds such as public pension funds are important in this discussion. From a perspective of domestic financial investment, two aspects set resource funds apart from these other funds.

First, resource funds are capitalized mainly by fiscal revenues largely arising from exports. As previously discussed, the domestic use of revenues that originate from abroad can lead to macroeconomic instability, exchange rate volatility and appreciation of the currency, and asset inflation. Furthermore, the risk of procyclicality extends to domestic financial investment by resource funds. During resource revenue downturns, if the budget comes under pressure, the fund's operations are not *de facto* independent, and its assets are relatively liquid, the fund might be called upon to help finance the budget, thereby forcing it to procyclically liquidate DFAs.

Second, the political economy of resource funds shows important differences with that of other publicly owned investment funds. Resource funds do not need to raise capital in financial markets, and they do not rely on pension contributions or (at least directly) on taxes that affect a significant share of the electorate. The lack of a strong constituency, such as pension contributors or lenders, combined with the conflicts of interest arising from the government's combined role as owner of the fund and promoter of its investments, make resource funds highly vulnerable to political interference. Political meddling can in turn put the wealth objectives of the funds, as well as the quality of domestic investments, at risk. Funds may be captured by political factions and used to avoid parliamentary scrutiny of spending on politically motivated projects.

Additional risk is generated if the fund's domestic investment mandate is defined to include development objectives, or economic externalities. An infrastructure project may provide beneficial externalities, such as the stimulation of private investments and jobs, which are not fully captured by its financial return. Economic externalities, however, are notoriously hard to measure. If the performance of fund management cannot be assessed on the basis of the fund's financial performance, assessment becomes difficult, which can increase the fund's vulnerability to political interference. In particular, funds could be used to bypass constraints on budget spending, and an increasing share of their portfolio could become inappropriate for a resource fund (Gelb, Tordo, and Halland 2014).

Therefore, while resource funds' domestic financial investment may open up new possibilities, the approach also carries very significant risks. These risks can hardly be eliminated. Can they be mitigated and managed? Gelb, Tordo, and Halland (2014) and Halland, Noel, and Tordo (forthcoming 2016) provide the following suggestions:

- The fund should not invest in public-policy-motivated projects justified primarily by their economic or social externalities and cannot be expected to generate a commercial financial return. Those projects should be in the budget.
- Domestic financial investments would instead be limited to undertakings with commercial financial returns. Where the fund invests with strategic objectives, it needs to maintain a market-based discipline so that those objectives be subordinated to the maximization of risk-adjusted financial returns and/or commercially based hurdle rates of return. This would preserve an intergenerational wealth transfer function for the fund. Wherever viability gaps exist that would have to be covered by subsidies, those subsidies would need to go through the budget.
- Fund integrity can be strengthened, and risks of political interference in asset allocation decisions reduced, by careful design of fund structure, investment policy, and domiciliation.
- The fund's management responsible for the investment portfolio should have legal and functional independence—to enable it to operate as a professional investment entity within its government-defined mandate.
- The fund needs to be staffed with highly skilled and experienced investment professionals. If the fund uses external investment managers, it would still need to build highly specialized capacity to contract and oversee the external managers.
- The fund's domestic financial investment needs to be considered within the overall macroeconomic framework. There is otherwise the risk that the fund would rapidly scale up investments when resource prices and revenues are high, contributing to Dutch disease, undermining efforts at countercyclical fiscal policy, and imposing costs on other investors. Fiscal risks arising from fund operations need to be assessed and controlled.
- The fund ought to undertake direct or portfolio domestic investments only as a minority shareholder, thereby leveraging private investment to bring in expertise and share project risk. This would reduce the risk of investment decisions being subject to political interference.
- Strong external and internal governance and transparent reporting, as well as independent and qualified audit, are crucial prerequisites. The fund's

governance needs to be based on a clear separation of responsibilities between the ownership role of the government, usually represented by the ministry of finance (MoF), the supervisory role of the fund's board, and the operational role of the fund's management.

Sometimes, distinguishing the operations of funds with commercial and asset value maximization objectives from funds that carry out public-policy-oriented investment may be complex (Shields and Villafuerte 2010). A key issue is the ability to assess the purpose and nature of fund operations. Moreover, the character of those operations or of fund orientation may evolve with time, as circumstances or politics change.

For example, some investments that turn out to be profitable may have been initially undertaken because of policy motives. Conversely, funds initially set to be managed on commercial and asset value maximization principles may, if these principles are not firmly anchored in legislation and practice, subsequently succumb to political pressures for directed financial investment, public spending, or lending for noncommercial purposes.

Institutional Arrangements for the Fund

The establishment of a fund entails decisions about how it is going to be integrated with the fiscal framework, the budget process, and asset and liability management. These decisions in turn have implications for institutional arrangements. Depending on its institutional design and mandate, a resource fund may help or hinder the budget system in meeting its basic objectives. This section will successively cover "virtual" funds, extrabudgetary resource funds, and the subset of these funds that undertake domestic operations.

The existence of a stabilization or savings fund need not imply the creation of a new institutional mechanism. A "fund" may be a fund in name only. This accounting-only design is referred to as a "virtual" fund, because there is no separate institutional structure for the management of the fund. Certain resources would be identified as belonging to the fund, and could be held in the government's main account, or in a separate government account with the central bank.

Alternatively, resource funds may be extrabudgetary funds with their own management, specific procedures, and accounts. Important PFM good practice principles for all extrabudgetary funds, including resource funds, include the following (Allen 2013; Shields 2013):

- Data on the fund require consolidation with other government financial information for the purposes of fiscal analysis and presentation of information in fiscal reports.
- Detailed accounts and other information on fund operations ought to be included in budget documentation to foster fiscal transparency; requirements for the classification of fund revenue and expenditure, accounting,

reporting, control, and audit ought to be established using either the budget system or comparable parallel procedures.

- Projections for the fund should be presented to the legislature as part of the budget process.

The degree of coordination required between the government (fiscal and monetary authorities) and the fund will depend on how much independence is granted to the fund's management, and to what extent the fund's investments are predetermined. In particular, a statutorily independent resource fund with discretion over its spending will need to keep the government informed of its spending intentions, so that the government can take appropriate supportive or offsetting action if needed (Shields 2013).

Resource funds that undertake domestic operations raise some further issues. As discussed above, funds that spend or invest domestically for public policy purposes need to be distinguished from funds that invest in DFAs for commercial and asset management reasons or with a "double bottom line" return criterion. From an institutional perspective, this distinction concerns, in particular, the degree of budget integration and the independence of the fund.

Resource funds that invest or spend domestically to carry out public policies require close integration with the budget. This is key to maintain overall coherence and integrity of public spending and fiscal policy. Given the quasi-fiscal nature of the operations of these funds, close integration with the budget process is required to avoid expenditure fragmentation, preserve unified fiscal control, and ensure consistent prioritization across government operations. In addition to the points above, this would involve, at least, the following:

- Budget formulation, MTEFs, and fiscal reporting should focus on a consolidated presentation (including the operations of the fund), to provide an accurate and comprehensive picture of public finances for fiscal policy formulation and assessment.
- All fund spending is best executed by the treasury to avoid duplicate processes.

Resource funds managed on a statutory and demonstrated commercial basis may be granted greater independence, subject to strong reporting and audit requirements. The management entities of funds that invest part of their financial assets domestically on purely commercial grounds—for portfolio management and asset value maximization purposes—would exercise independence in making investment decisions, free from political interference, under the mandate provided by the government. In these cases, only the overall domestic financial investment envelope would be coordinated with the budget (for macroeconomic management purposes). The fund would need to provide transparent and independent reporting of results, with internal and external audits. Similar considerations apply for funds with a "double trigger" investment criterion but checks and balances may need to be even stronger for this category—particularly in weak-governance contexts where political interference with investment decisions is otherwise likely.

A number of governments, for example, in Alberta, Algeria, Azerbaijan, Chile, Kazakhstan, and Mexico, have made efforts in recent years to improve the functioning of their funds. Reforms have generally moved in the direction of simplification, better integration of the funds with budget systems and fiscal policy frameworks, and the strengthening of fiscal transparency.

A resource fund can hold a significant share of the public sector's financial resources and be an important element of the government's overall asset and liability management structure. Readers interested in resource fund asset management issues are referred to IMF (2012e, 2014h), Das, Mazarei, and van der Hoorn (2010), Al-Hassan and others (2013), Shields (2013), and Megginson and Fotak (2016).

Governance, Transparency, and Accountability

Lessons from experience and best practice suggest that good governance of a fund and strong transparency are important for the achievement of its objectives. The objectives and mandate of the fund, the organization of the ownership function of the state, and the institutional arrangements that govern its internal management bodies and processes are usually specified in a purpose-designed law, as well as company law, financial sector regulations, and the fund's statutes. The *Santiago Principles* for the operations of SWFs (IWGS 2008, see appendix E), the Revised Guidelines for Foreign Exchange Reserve Management (IMF 2013d), and existing literature on good corporate governance practice, including the *Principles of Corporate Governance* (OECD 2004), and the *Guidelines on Corporate Governance of State Owned Enterprises* (OECD 2006) provide a detailed framework for effective corporate governance. According to Gelb, Tordo, and Halland (2014) governance can be separated into external and internal arrangements:

External governance relates to the relationship between the fund and the state as its owner. Ownership provides certain rights and obligations, including voting on matters defined by law and by the fund's statutes; electing, appointing, and removing board members; and obtaining information on the performance of the fund, its board, and its management.

Internal governance includes institutional arrangements, such as the composition, structure, functioning, and authority of the board of directors or trustees, and the fund's management processes, including recruitment, decision making, raising capital, investment autonomy, risk management, asset classes, audit, and public disclosures.

Good governance and transparency are key to:

• *Garner public support for the fund and its objectives.* Society is more likely to support arrangements for the accumulation of potentially significant country assets when it is provided with reliable information about the management and evolution of those assets and when it can exert pressure for good asset management. Lack of transparency can hamper legitimacy and fetter public support for the fund.

- *Enhance fund performance.* Transparency fosters accountability to the public, thereby providing incentives for the fund's management to maximize returns subject to their mandate, and run the fund with integrity.
- *Help prevent political capture, mismanagement, corruption, and abuse.* This is particularly important given the magnitude of the public resources that may be at stake.

Strong vertical and horizontal accountability and transparency will enhance the effectiveness and efficiency of the fund. Petersen and Budina (2003) and Heilbrunn (2002) stress the importance of vertical and horizontal accountability:

- *Vertical accountability.* The fund's management is subject to hierarchical oversight and is answerable to a higher authority, which in turn is answerable to an elected higher authority. This involves clear lines of responsibility and regular reporting.
- *Horizontal accountability.* The operations and performance of the fund are overseen by other government agencies (including audit) and are reported to civil society.

Against this background, and more specifically:

- The framework for the resource fund needs to be set up and supported by legislation.
- Clear lines of responsibility and accountability are required between the owner (usually represented by the MoF) and the manager of the fund.
  - The owner of the fund has overall responsibility and sets out strategic investment guidelines and evaluates operational management.
  - The manager of the fund implements the investment strategy set out by the owner, manages risk within the permitted parameters, and ensures proper accounting and reporting according to the regulations.
- Openness is critical and involves the public disclosure of fund objectives, regulations, investment strategies, and accountability structure, as well as periodic and timely public reports on fund performance and disclosure of fund assets.
- Control and evaluation mechanisms include parliamentary oversight, performance assessment, and independent internal and external audit.

Suggestions for Resource Fund Design

The rationale for a resource fund must be carefully considered on a case-by-case basis. What would the fund help do better than established budget and asset management systems? Do the potential benefits outweigh the potential costs?

SSFs with rigid operational rules are best avoided. While the advantages of these funds in stabilizing expenditure or promoting saving are uncertain because money is fungible, they may hamper effective fiscal and asset management and often entail costs.

Financing funds with flexible rules are preferred. These funds do not impose inefficiencies and rigidities on fiscal policy and asset/liability management. They devolve the focus of fiscal policy design and implementation to the budget. They can also help highlight the importance of the NRB for fiscal programming.

Good integration with budget systems and fiscal policy frameworks is best achieved by ensuring that the fund does not interfere with PFM processes and ensures coherent asset and liability management.

The operations of the fund and its financial assets and liabilities should be reported regularly to the government, disclosed in fund and government financial statements, and be subject to internal and external audit.

In resource-rich countries the first-best approach is not to grant spending authority for public policy purposes to the fund and to preserve the integrity of the budget. This suggestion arises from sound PFM principles, consideration of the nature of resource revenue, political economy issues, and the evidence from country experience. It would be better to tackle existing PFM shortcomings head on, rather than attempt to bypass them through a spending fund.

Funds with authority to spend off-budget for public policy purposes need to be closely integrated with the budget process. This is critical to ensure holistic expenditure prioritization, avoid policy fragmentation, and preserve unified fiscal control. The fund should be included in a consolidated budget submitted to the legislature, and its operations and plans discussed in budget documents. This is needed for an informed consideration of the overall fiscal position.

Funds with authority to invest domestically on commercial principles, as part of their asset management strategies, or with a "double bottom line" investment criterion, need to be allowed to carry out their mandates independently, and be required to transparently report their operations. Fund management—charged with the maximization of fund asset value subject to tolerable risk as mandated by the government—requires independence from political interference. At the same time, they must be held accountable for fund performance. The operations of the fund need to be reported in budget documents.

Stringent mechanisms to ensure transparency, governance, and accountability are key requirements for resource funds. Rigorous procedures need to be in place to help prevent misuse of public resources and provide assurance that government assets are properly and prudently managed.

Notes

1. Resource-rich countries that have, or have had, resource funds include the following (countries marked with * also have, or have had, a fiscal rule or guideline): Algeria, Angola, Azerbaijan*, Bahrain, Botswana, Brunei, Chad*, Chile, Ecuador*, Gabon, Ghana*, Equatorial Guinea*, the Islamic Republic of Iran, Kazakhstan, Kuwait, Libya, Mexico*, Mongolia*, Nigeria*, Norway*, Oman, Papua New Guinea, Qatar, Russia*, Sudan, Timor-Leste*, Trinidad and Tobago, the United Arab Emirates, and República Bolivariana de Venezuela.* The State of Alaska and the province of Alberta* also have funds. New resource funds are expected to be set up in some resource-rich countries. Bacon and Tordo (2006) offer a review of a number of resource funds.

2. The lists provide examples of countries that have implemented certain types of resource funds, either in the past or present. The inclusion of a country in a certain category does not necessarily imply that the fund with the particular operational rules indicated is currently in place—the fund may have been in place in the past and subsequently its rules may have been changed, or it may have been eliminated.

3. Money is fungible because its individual units are equivalent and thus amenable to mutual substitution.

CHAPTER 9

Revenue Earmarking

Revenue earmarking is the practice of assigning revenue from certain specified taxes or from general revenue to specific expenditures or to broad expenditure areas, through law or constitutional clauses (Ruiz 2010). Some resource-rich countries have formally earmarked certain revenues, or shares of total revenue, to specific spending categories, and some have minimum spending requirements—formulated, for example, as minimum expenditure ratios to gross domestic product (GDP). These procedures sometimes take place through extrabudgetary funds and resource funds charged with earmarked or protected spending.

Revenue earmarking can in some cases be justified and may be beneficial. The benefit principle of taxation is the classic argument to justify earmarking on efficiency grounds. Under this principle, those who benefit from the consumption of a publicly provided good should pay for it. According to Shah (2007), earmarking revenue for specific expenditures is acceptable only when there is a direct link between the two, such as road taxes to finance road maintenance. There are international examples of successful limited earmarking in the areas of social security and special sectors, such as water and sewerage (Ruiz 2010). The discussion that follows focuses on situations of extensive revenue earmarking, where the sources of funding and the expenditures funded are unrelated, with fiscal and macroeconomic implications.

There are various motivations for earmarking revenue. Different governments have resorted to earmarking for different reasons, including to (i) improve resource allocation; (ii) ensure the funding of expenditures that are traditionally vulnerable or neglected in the budget process (such as road maintenance); (iii) address time-consistency problems (future governments may neglect some expenditures); (iv) "protect" temporary revenues, such as resource revenue or privatization receipts, assign them to perceived appropriate uses, and avoid permanent increases in spending; (v) prevent the inappropriate use of resource revenue; (vi) ensure the financial autonomy of some institutions; and (vii) facilitate politically the introduction of new taxes or increases in tax rates or broadening of the bases of existing taxes by earmarking the proceeds from these measures to expenditures broadly supported by the public.

Revenue earmarking, however, can also be a manifestation of the breakdown of standard budget allocation processes and of complex political economy dynamics. When the allocation of resources through competition in the budget is dysfunctional or is not trusted, or when powerful groups hijack the political process, vested interests can capture public resources through earmarking. Pressure groups, with little trust in the budget process, act on the principle "I grab before you grab."

This can be particularly acute in resource-rich countries, where competition for large resource rents can weaken institutions and agencies of restraint. For any given pressure group, rents divert incentives away from ensuring efficient use of resources across the economy (including by other groups) in favor of appropriating and earmarking rents unencumbered by the reciprocal scrutiny of other groups (Eifert, Gelb, and Tallroth 2003).

There is a slippery slope associated with the precedent of introducing earmarking for one or a few sectors. Other ministries or pressure groups can subsequently use the earmarking granted to justify their own right to earmarked revenues. A noncooperative game ensues, as a result of which all groups may well end up worse off. And earmarking, once established, typically becomes entrenched and is difficult to eliminate.

Most public finance economists are skeptical about earmarking beyond the cases noted at the beginning of this chapter. They are of the view that the benefits are outweighed by the negative impact of earmarking on budget management. By this line of argument, revenue earmarking contravenes fundamental public financial management (PFM) principles, including single-point decision making on overall expenditure and the common pool principle for managing budget resources (Fainboim 2009).

In practice, extensive revenue earmarking has often had negative effects. For example, budget rigidities, including revenue earmarking and mandatory expenditure requirements, have constrained fiscal management and reduced the efficiency of public expenditure in a number of Latin American countries. By the mid-2000s, the International Monetary Fund (IMF) considered that lack of budget flexibility ranked high among the most pressing problems faced by Latin American budgetary authorities (IMF 2006b; see also Cetrángolo and Jiménez 2009; Alier, undated). Ruiz (2010) discusses the problems associated with extensive revenue earmarking in Central America.

Governments considering earmarking would be well advised to take into account the problems that it can create for the efficient allocation of resources, fiscal policy, PFM, and macrostability:

Earmarking hampers the efficient allocation of resources and weakens incentives to improve spending efficiency. The link between the amount of resources earmarked to an activity and the actual needs in the area may be tenuous. If too much is transferred, there are no incentives to use resources efficiently, waste ensues, and/

or idle deposits build up. If too little is transferred, worthy needs may go unmet. It also does not make sense to earmark specific shares of highly volatile resource revenue or total revenue to specific spending categories, because expenditure priorities and needs are uncorrelated with the vagaries of resource revenue and are likely to benefit from funding stability.

For example, in Chile, 10 percent of the gross copper revenue of the national copper company is earmarked for defense expenditure. The earmark used, a very volatile revenue, exacerbates the divorce between sectorial needs and funding. Chile's defense budget received growing resources as the copper boom got under way during the 2000s. As expenditure nonetheless lagged behind rapidly rising copper revenue (constrained by the government to comply with the structural balance [SB] guideline), the sector accumulated large financial assets (Fainboim 2009). The government has since committed to the reform of defense financing.

Earmarking reduces budget flexibility, and limits the reallocation of public resources in response to changing needs. The resources given to an earmarked activity may have had more efficient and effective uses elsewhere. This can be a source of frustration to governments that cannot find fiscal space for implementing new priority programs.

For example, Chad and Ecuador addressed previous problems caused by revenue earmarking. Prior to the reforms, in both countries resources that were transferred to budget entities, to comply with mandatory revenue earmarking provisions, remained unspent and idle, while arrears to suppliers or in priority sectors mounted, due to treasury cash-flow difficulties. Chad modified its earmarking system to allow greater expenditure flexibility in 2006. Ecuador eliminated most revenue earmarking—and all resource revenue earmarking—in 2008 (Cueva 2008; Dabán and Hélis 2010; Villafuerte, López-Murphy, and Ossowski 2010).

Earmarking can complicate fiscal adjustment and hamper its quality. First, fiscal adjustments based on revenue increases may require larger increases in taxes than would be the case without earmarking, because part of the new revenues may need to be allocated to the sectors favored by revenue earmarking. Second, in fiscal adjustments that include expenditure reductions, the cuts have to be borne by the sectors not favored by earmarking, as the latter will be automatically sheltered. Since public investment is one of the most important discretionary spending categories, it is likely to be one of the sectors affected by revenue earmarking in expenditure consolidations, with the negative implications discussed earlier in this volume.

Earmarking can distort tax policy choices and lead to a built-in bias toward higher taxation and spending. The application of earmarking and/or of different earmarks to different taxes can influence the choice of tax policies. For example, in Argentina in 2001 the government introduced a financial transactions tax creditable against value added tax (VAT) and income tax obligations. The existing taxes were subject to earmarking and shared with the provinces, whereas the new tax initially was not (Cuevas 2003). In Brazil, tax policy has been influenced by revenue earmarking and the system of intergovernmental transfers, as these mechanisms apply only to certain categories of taxes (Ter-Minassian 2012).

Earmarking can hamper efficient cash management. In Algeria, oil accounts allocated to multiyear public investment projects, complicated cash management and undermined transparency and accountability (Dabán and Hélis 2010).

Earmarking can contribute to public expenditure creep. In Brazil, minimum spending requirements that apply to health and education and pervasive revenue earmarking may have contributed to the strong growth in current expenditure in the last couple of decades (Ter-Minassian 2012).

Earmarking can contribute to procyclicality in public spending. In the absence of a stabilization mechanism, earmarked resources assigned to the favored spending areas rise and fall with government revenues. In resource-rich countries earmarking resource revenue is particularly procyclical and transfers resource volatility to the nonresource sector. Moreover, the sectors favored by earmarking such as social spending need stable and predictable funding.

For example, in Colombia (where fiscal oil dependence is moderate), revenue earmarking, although declining, still makes up a very large share of the budget. Estimates suggest that in 2013 the share of earmarked expenditures of the general government ranged from 61 percent to 80 percent (OECD and IDB 2014). This contributed to fiscal policy procyclicality and hampered fiscal adjustments (Echeverry, Navas, and Clavijo 2009).

Earmarking can complicate fiscal management without necessarily achieving its intended results. In countries where new resource discoveries are made it is sometimes thought that the new revenues should be earmarked to "worthy" expenditures, possibly through resource funds, to prevent them from being used inappropriately. Whether this result will be achieved, however, is uncertain because money is fungible. The new revenues may be earmarked to the "worthy" expenditures, but as the example in table 9.1 shows, a parallel increase in inappropriate spending can take place by reducing other spending if liquidity constraints are binding (alternative 1 in the table 9.1) or by borrowing or running down assets if there are no liquidity constraints (alternative 2). In situations of new resource discoveries, with resource revenue rising rapidly, liquidity is unlikely to be a serious issue.

In other words, earmarking is not enough to prevent inappropriate spending. Political will is required to not undo elsewhere in the budget what is being done through earmarking. And if the political will to spend appropriately exists, the rationale for earmarking may not necessarily be clear.

Earmarking can hamper an appropriate implementation of a medium-term expenditure framework (MTEF). The expenditure rigidities it entails and the volatility it imparts to spending in resource-rich countries can conflict with the expenditure flexibility and stability that are among the fundamental objectives of MTEFs.

In some cases where the expenditure allocation processes and PFM are weak, specific types of earmarking have been proposed as the only way to ensure

Table 9.1 Revenue Earmarking: A Potentially Ineffective Way to Prevent Inappropriate Spending

	Desired		Alternative 1		Alternative 2	
	T	T+1	T	T+1	T	T+1
Revenue	**100**	**103**	**100**	**103**	**100**	**103**
Resource revenue (earmarked)	0	3	0	3	0	3
Nonresource revenue	100	100	100	100	100	100
Expenditure	**100**	**103**	**100**	**103**	**100**	**106**
"Appropriate"	100	103	100	100	100	103
Financed by earmarked revenue	0	3	0	3	0	3
Other	100	100	100	97	100	100
"Inappropriate"	0	0	0	3	0	3
Balance	**0**	**0**	**0**	**0**	**0**	**−3**

minimum allocations to critical expenditure items, such as health and education, that may be neglected in the budget process. In some countries, minimum expenditure requirements (without earmarking) have been established. Under such provisions, constitutional or legal requirements mandate to devote certain shares of spending to specified expenditure categories, or to increase spending on those categories, in line with an indexation factor such as nominal GDP.

These mechanisms may improve the availability of resources to the favored sectors. Whether this happens or not will depend in part on whether the PFM system, including budget accounting and classification systems, is robust to withstand the likely attempts at misclassifying spending and other ways to get around earmarking or minimum spending requirements, as money is fungible. On the other hand, the potential macroeconomic, fiscal, and efficiency costs of these mechanisms have already been discussed above.

Revenue earmarking motivated by concerns about the availability of resources to sectors neglected in the budget process could be made temporary, with sunset clauses, pending improvements in budget allocation systems. Such palliatives, however, may reduce the urgency of desirable and better reforms in budget formulation. There is also a risk that the mechanisms become entrenched and difficult to abolish when the time comes—policy measures with an initially temporary time frame, such as some tax increases at times of fiscal crisis in some countries, have not infrequently been extended in time.

The transfer of shares of central government resource revenues or of general revenues to the resource-producing regions when resource revenue is assigned by the constitution or law to the central government, while a form of revenue earmarking, is in fact a fiscal federalism and intergovernmental relations issue. Discussion of the highly complex and multidimensional issues involved in this topic lies outside the scope of this volume. Interested readers are referred to the literature mentioned at the end of chapter 2.

Some resource funds have had part of their resources earmarked for specific purposes. Objectives have varied. For example, in Alaska the dividend program from the Alaska Permanent Fund was established in part to foster a constituency supportive of the oil fund. This was achieved: the population has consistently opposed using the fund's capital to finance expenditures. But spending was sometimes financed with debt. And the dividends paid to the population from the fund's income became deeply entrenched entitlements that did not compete with other spending needs (see appendix D). In Chad and Ecuador, objectives included making it easier to resist political pressures to use oil revenue inappropriately, and prioritizing the use of resources for special purposes, such as poverty reduction or debt service. The experience was not positive, as discussed above.

In short, while some well-defined and limited revenue earmarking can be justified in the circumstances discussed at the beginning of this chapter, in general it makes little sense to earmark shares of highly volatile resource revenue or total revenue to specific spending categories. Expenditure priorities and needs are likely to benefit from funding stability and predictability, they are uncorrelated with the vagaries of resource revenue, and earmarking imparts procyclicality to fiscal policy.

Strategies are available to limit or reduce revenue earmarking. A discussion of the extent and costs of existing revenue earmarking in budget documents and MTEFs can be useful. Besides the need for transparency, from a political economy point of view, disclosure might help develop constituencies over time in support of greater budget flexibility. Introducing institutional mechanisms for the periodic assessment of earmarking, and its gradual reduction, can be helpful. Such analyses may show, for example, that old-vintage earmarking may no longer be relevant. Legislation prohibiting new earmarking can also be useful. Finally, if revenue earmarking is removed and depending on the circumstances, the spending sectors affected may need to be sheltered from sudden declines in financing.

CHAPTER 10

The Resource Price, or Revenue, in the Budget

Forecasting resource revenue accurately is a significant challenge for resource-rich countries. Developments in resource markets in the past few years make clear the high volatility of spot resource prices. Moreover, the record of expert forecasts and futures prices to predict price movements and future prices is very poor (figure 1.2). Forecasts from international agencies and futures prices have routinely missed abrupt changes in spot prices and been way off target. Some resource-rich countries also have a poor record in projecting resource output volumes, even in the short term, a point that is perhaps less widely realized.

Countries use a wide array of approaches to determine the reference resource price in the budget. As can be seen from box 10.1, many resource-rich countries

---

Box 10.1 The Resource Price in the Budget: Country Practices

In Chile, a panel of copper experts estimates every year a "long-run price of copper" that is used as input for the formulation of the next year's budget (Chile, Comité Asesor 2011; see appendix C).

Mexico uses a rolling formula based on a weighted average: the 10-year historical average oil price with a weight of 25 percent; medium-term futures prices with a weight of 25 percent; and short-term futures prices (with a discount factor to provide some protection against downside risks) with a weight of 50 percent (IMF 2012a).

In Nigeria, the budget reference oil price has been set low, relative to oil market prices, and bargaining between the federal government and the legislature has played an important role in its determination (IMF 2013e).

Angola and some other African oil exporters have used the International Monetary Fund's (IMF's) *World Economic Outlook* (WEO) oil price projections less a discount (Watson 2011).

---

box continues next page

Box 10.1 The Resource Price in the Budget: Country Practices *(continued)*

Timor-Leste uses the average of the U.S. Energy Information Administration's low case and the reference case Brent crude price (Timor-Leste 2014).

In the Middle East and North Africa (MENA), conservative oil prices have tended to be set on an ad hoc basis (Watson 2011).

In República Bolivariana de Venezuela, the reference oil price for the budget has typically been underestimated (Manzano and others 2012).

In Norway, the oil price forecast is of no consequence to the annual budget: spending is fully decoupled from current oil revenues, and the budget targets the non-oil structural balance; any conceivable budget deficit in a given year can easily be financed from the resources in the Government Pension Fund-Global (GPF-G).

Source: Authors, based on sources noted in box.

---

have tended to use conservative resource price or revenue forecasts to determine the budget's resource envelope. Often these forecasts have turned out to be underestimates, as was observed during the period of rising resource prices in the 2000s. There are various reasons why a government might set a cautious resource price in the annual budget, and not all of them have to do with prudence.

A conservative resource price or revenue assumption is often seen as a prudent way to reduce the risk of a large deficit or fiscal adjustment in the event of an unanticipated decline in resource revenue. This assumes asymmetric adjustment costs. This is an example of a more general tendency for revenue forecasters to produce conservative rather than expected revenue estimates when the short-term budget position is not buttressed by stabilization mechanisms that could be used in the event of revenue shortfalls, such as contingency and reserve funds, and availability of credit (Glenday 2013).

Some governments have used low budget resource prices in an attempt to contain spending pressures. Showing less resources in the budget might help dampen spending enthusiasm. In some cases, governments have felt it politically difficult to propose budgets where a "realistic" resource price forecast combined with spending plans results in a projected budget surplus.

In some cases, low budget resource prices have also been used at least partly in an attempt to limit formula-based revenue sharing with subnational governments (SNGs)—as in Nigeria and República Bolivariana de Venezuela. In the case of Nigeria, in recent years the low budget oil price was driven primarily by fiscal consolidation objectives and to increase deposits in the Excess Crude Account (ECA), and also to generate an ex-ante fiscal deficit, in part to try and enforce spending discipline on SNGs, which have limited borrowing capacity (IMF 2013e). In República Bolivariana de Venezuela, revenue sharing with SNGs is based on the approved budget, and the rules to transfer additional revenues during budget execution are not well defined. Hence the central government benefits from underestimating the oil price (Manzano and others 2012).

The use of artificially low resource prices to try and restrain spending, however, is likely to be challenged—it will not necessarily deliver lower spending and is unlikely to be sustainable for long. Legislatures and pressure groups eventually see through it and learn to play the strategic game with the government. In Mexico, for example, prior to the reform that mandated setting the oil price in the budget through a transparent formula, the oil price used in the budget was negotiated with congress (IMF 2005d).

The resource revenue in the budget can be set strategically low so that there is a high probability that revenues come in higher during budget execution, to allow the discretionary allocation of the extra revenues to additional spending not in the budget, on an ad-hoc basis and sometimes bypassing budget processes and oversight. In some oil-exporting countries (OECs) oil revenues in excess of budget projections have been routinely used to increase budget spending or to finance off-budget expenditures during the fiscal year, with little oversight. This damaging practice often resulted in procyclical, poorly planned, and inefficient spending that did not meet contestability tests, undermining fiscal transparency and the integrity and credibility of the budget.

Suggestions for the Resource Price or Revenue Used in Budgets

Resource revenue projections in the budget need to be unbiased, realistic, credible, and transparent. Safety from risk should not be sought in an artificially low resource price: it should be sought in budgeting expenditure prudently and by including contingencies. While acknowledging the enormous uncertainty surrounding forecasts, a reasonable procedure is to use market forecast prices adjusted for quality and transport costs, perhaps combining them with independent expert forecasts. Expenditure can be risk adjusted to cover eventualities. The budget can include stress testing of the proposed fiscal position to downturns in resource revenue and potential mitigation strategies, to facilitate an informed evaluation of risks.

The use of long, backward-looking, moving average price formulas to set the budget price is not justified. As discussed earlier, given the nature of the stochastic process driving resource prices and substantial persistence of shocks, prices set by such formulas are likely to overshoot or undershoot spot prices for years. Simple simulations using historical prices confirm this feature of moving average formulas, which are quickly understood by legislatures and pressure groups.

Budget amendment procedures need to be transparent and require compliance. In light of the resource revenue forecast errors that inevitably occur, it is vital in resource-rich countries to have stringent procedures to amend the budget during execution if necessary, and to submit final execution reports to the relevant audit offices and to parliament. The procedures need to preclude undertaking additional expenditures during the year without proper ex-ante appropriation, consistent with the country's budget systems law or equivalent, or undertaking off-budget spending.

The practice of raising spending during the year is, in any event, incompatible with a medium-term expenditure framework. Framing expenditure in a multi-year context prevents opportunistic spending increases if revenues are higher than expected in a given year.

Arguably, an important policy objective for countries would be to reach a position where the annual budget becomes less dependent on the particular resource price projection for the budget year. This requires three things. First, a strong financial position so that the budget is not vulnerable to the resource price in the very short term (one to two years). Second, targeting the nonresource balance or nonresource primary balance with expenditure decoupled from short-term resource price movements, ex-ante and during budget execution (which may require stabilization arrangements if there are formula-based intergovernmental transfers to SNGs). Third, a strong medium- and long-term perspective for fiscal policy in which the annual budget is embedded. If resource prices change on a sustained basis, fiscal policy can be reassessed in an orderly manner in the context of medium- and long-term fiscal plans, as required.

Indicators for Fiscal Analysis in Resource-Rich Countries

A number of indicators are available for the analysis of fiscal policy in resource-rich countries. The special characteristics of resource revenue and their implications for short- and long-run fiscal policy in these countries require that attention be given to several fiscal indicators to interpret the impact of fiscal policy appropriately and enhance fiscal planning.

In resource-rich countries the *overall balance (net lending/borrowing)* and the *primary balance* used as key fiscal indicators in other countries do not adequately assess the impact of fiscal policy on domestic demand. This is because they do not take into account the specific nature of resource revenue. Since such revenue largely originates from abroad, unlike domestic taxes, its effect on the purchasing power of domestic economic agents is limited. Changes in the primary or overall fiscal balance arising from pure fluctuations in resource revenue should be expected to have limited short-term effects on domestic demand.

A rising overall balance could easily mask an expansionary or unsustainable fiscal policy stance, and be incorrectly interpreted as a tightening of fiscal policy. If the government decides to spend a resource revenue windfall, expenditures can rise without either a deterioration in the overall balance, or the imposition of additional tax burdens. Higher government spending would, however, add to demand pressures, including on imports. This effect would not be picked up by the overall balance, which indeed could improve with rising resource revenue at the same time that fiscal policy is actually loosened by spending some of the additional resource revenue. Conversely, a deterioration in the overall balance because of lower resource revenue may mask significant adjustment efforts, as the example of Angola in 2009 (mentioned in chapter 1) or of a number of countries in 2015 (chapter 2) illustrates.

The *nonresource balance* (NRB) and the *nonresource primary balance* (NRPB) provide more accurate indicators of the underlying fiscal position in the short run and of the impact of fiscal policy on domestic demand:

- The NRB is the difference between nonresource revenues and nonresource expenditures.[1] It abstracts from revenue fluctuations caused by changes in international resource prices, resource production volumes and costs, and other resource-related factors. The NRB is also a reasonable proxy for the injection of resource revenue into the economy.[2]
- The NRPB is the NRB that, in addition, also excludes investment income on government assets and interest payments on government liabilities. These fiscal flows are, at least in the short run, not under the control of the government, and in many resource-rich countries they largely accrue from, or are paid to, foreign residents—and to that extent do not affect the disposable income of domestic economic agents.
- The NRB and NRPB also provide a measure of fiscal vulnerability. If expenditures have increased during a period of rising resource revenue, the resulting higher nonresource deficit may be difficult to finance in a downturn, or become unsustainable in the absence of a compensating fiscal or exchange rate adjustment to the lower resource revenue.
- Moreover, the main indicator of the fiscal position for sustainability analyses in resource-rich countries (equivalent to the primary balance in other countries) is the NRPB. This indicator makes explicit that, from a sustainability point of view, fiscal revenue should exclude nonrenewable resource income on the grounds that it is more like financing—a transformation of assets from exhaustible resource reserves in the ground to other assets. And when the nonrenewable resource has been exhausted or has been rendered obsolete, the NRPB converges to the primary balance used in traditional sustainability analysis in other countries.

The *domestic balance* may be used to more accurately identify the direct impact of the government on the domestic economy. It includes only those components of the overall balance that arise from transactions with the domestic economy, and omits those transactions directly affecting the balance of payments, such as government imports. This balance, however, may be difficult to compute. The breakdown of government expenditure into its domestic and foreign components may not be feasible due to lack of sufficient information. For operational purposes, the NRPB will often be a reasonable proxy for the domestic balance.

The *overall balance* is a good indicator of the government's net financing requirement, changes in net financial assets, and fiscal vulnerability. The evaluation of a particular overall balance will require assessment of the fiscal and macroeconomic impact of alternative methods of financing it. For example, the domestic financing of an overall deficit may be inflationary, or may crowd out private sector investment, while external financing may be too costly or unavailable.

Table A.1 illustrates the derivation of the NRB, the NRPB, and the overall balance by means of an example derived from the Republic of Congo's central government operations in 2013, as reported in IMF (2014j).

The *gross borrowing requirement* (GBR) is an important indicator in resource-rich countries where the financial position of the government is particularly weak and there are short-term financing concerns. The GBR is defined as the overall deficit plus gross amortization due during the period. In some countries with precarious fiscal positions, the volatile and uncertain nature of resource revenue requires undertaking sensitivity analyses of alternative resource revenue scenarios for the GBR. This is particularly important when market concerns about short-run liquidity and fiscal sustainability raise questions about the availability of credit to cover the government's financing needs.

Table A.1 Republic of Congo: Central Government Operations Estimated for 2013
percentage of non-oil GDP

		2013
Total revenue and grants	A	**111.7**
Primary revenue		110.7
Oil revenue	B	82.1
Non-oil revenue		28.6
Investment income	C	0.0
Grants		0.9
Expenditure and net lending	D	**91.4**
Current expenditure		33.7
Primary current expenditure		33.1
Oil-related expenditure	E	0.0
Other		33.1
Interest	F	0.6
Capital expenditure and net lending		57.7
Oil-related expenditure and net lending	G	0.0
Other		57.7
Non-oil balance[a]	**(A–B)–(D–E–G)**	**–61.8**
Non-oil primary balance[a]	**(A–B–C)–(D–E–F–G)**	**–61.2**
Overall balance (including grants)[a]	**A–D**	**20.3**
Financing		**–20.3**
Foreign (net)		–9.1
Disbursement		17.8
Amortization due		–5.6
Other[b]		–21.3
Domestic (net)[c]		–11.2

Source: Derived by the authors from table 4 in IMF (2014j).
Notes: GDP = gross domestic product.
[a] On a commitment basis.
[b] Includes change in deposits abroad.
[c] Includes change in domestic arrears.

Cyclically adjusted balances (CABs) and *structural balances (SBs)* are fiscal indicators adjusted for the economic cycle (in the case of the CAB) and for the cycle and other elements (for the SB). They are discussed in appendix B.

For the normalization of fiscal variables, nonresource gross domestic product (NRGDP) is a better scaling factor in resource-rich countries than is total GDP. In these countries, resource prices can have major effects on the observed ratios of fiscal variables to GDP, because the resource and nonresource GDP deflators often deviate markedly, making nominal GDP quite volatile. Volatile resource prices can drive large changes in nominal GDP, and therefore in conventional fiscal policy indicators expressed as ratios to GDP, that can make it quite difficult to interpret these ratios. For example, the ratio of nonresource revenue to total GDP may fluctuate because of volatility in resource GDP, even though the ratio of nonresource revenue to the nonresource taxable base or to NRGDP is stable.

Thus, the ratio of the NRB to NRGDP is a reliable and informative fiscal indicator for short- and long-term analysis and fiscal policy formulation in resource-rich countries (Barnett and Ossowski 2003; Medas and Zakharova 2009; Villafuerte and López-Murphy 2010; IMF 2012a). In addition to the overall balance (and the gross financing requirement, when financing is an issue), budget documents should include and discuss the NRB and NRPB.

Finally, *changes in expenditure in real terms* are also an important fiscal indicator in resource-rich countries. They will often be more informative than changes in the ratio of expenditure to GDP, which is affected by the volatility of nominal GDP mentioned above. They can usefully complement the analysis of the ratio of expenditure to NRGDP.

Notes

1. In some countries, budgets may include some resource-related expenditures, which should not be included in the nonresource balance (NRB). For instance, in Norway, the budget includes expenditures related to the state's participation in the oil sector. In Iran, oil export revenue accrues to the central government, and the latter transfers a share of those revenues to the national oil company, classified as expenditure.

2. The definition of what revenues constitute resource revenues may not be straightforward. In 2014, the International Monetary Fund (IMF) proposed for public consultation a standard template for data on government revenues from natural resources based on the revenue classification of the *Government Finance Statistics Manual 2001* (IMF 2014i).

Methodological Issues in the Assessment of Fiscal Policy Cyclicality in Resource-Rich Countries

The main purpose of cyclical adjustment is to arrive at an estimate of the government's underlying fiscal position. To this end, fiscal aggregates are adjusted for the economic cycle to estimate the underlying fiscal position net of cyclical effects—that is, what revenue, expenditure, and the balance would be if output were at its potential level—and to assess the discretionary fiscal policy contribution to demand (Escolano 2010; Bornhorst and others 2011).

- *Cyclically adjusted balances (CABs)* are computed by excluding those components that are due to a negative or positive output gap—that is, the difference between actual output and potential output. Fiscal policy is said to be *expansionary* when the change in the CAB is negative, and *contractionary* when it is positive. If the estimated change in the output gap during the period is positive, then expansionary fiscal policy is *procyclical*, and contractionary fiscal policy is *countercyclical*; and vice versa.
- *Structural balances (SBs)* are an extension of CABs. The International Monetary Fund's *World Economic Outlook* (IMF's WEO) defines SBs as the CABs adjusted further for nonstructural elements beyond the economic cycle, including, for example, financial sector and asset price movements, as well as temporary or one-off revenue or expenditure items.

Assessments of the cyclicality of fiscal policy in resource-rich countries are more challenging than in other countries, because they need to take into account the specific characteristics of fiscal resource revenue and their implications. As noted above, these fiscal revenues are more volatile and uncertain than other revenues; they largely originate from abroad, and they are injected into the economy through the nonresource fiscal deficit.

One way to estimate the SB in resource-rich countries is to distinguish between resource revenue and other revenues and attempt to estimate the "structural" level for each. The SB is then defined as the sum of structural resource revenues and structural nonresource revenues net of government expenditures.[1] The fiscal stance is then characterized as expansionary or contractionary by analyzing the changes in the estimated SB as a ratio to gross domestic product (GDP). Examples of this method as applied to Latin American countries can be found in, for example, Alberola and Montero (2006), Izquierdo and Talvi (2008), and Vladkova-Hollar and Zettelmeyer (2008).

This approach to estimating the SB suffers from some drawbacks. In particular, the "structural" level of resource revenue is subject to significant estimation uncertainty resulting from the nature of the stochastic process that drives resource prices and their high volatility, shock persistence, and unpredictability.[2] While there is no consensus on this issue, a body of expert opinion considers the process driving oil prices to be nonstationary, meaning that there may not be a well-defined "long-term average price" for oil. Empirical time-series analyses of resource prices typically show that shocks are highly persistent.

- In a detailed study of the statistical properties of oil prices, Engel and Valdés (2000) conclude that in terms of out-of-sample prediction power, no statistical model performs better than a random walk without drift.
- In a major study of oil prices, Hamilton (2008) also finds that the statistical evidence is consistent with the view that the price of oil in real terms seems to follow a random walk without drift. He emphasizes the enormous uncertainty surrounding oil price forecasts. Changes in the real price of oil have historically tended to be statistically permanent (that is, the persistence component in oil prices is very high relative to the temporary or mean-reverting component), difficult to predict, and governed by different regimes at different points in time.
- Based on an econometric study of a long time series, Brahmbhatt and Canuto (2010) conclude that real commodity prices do not display any trend or drift over time, and that it is not possible to reject the unit root hypothesis for these prices.
- In contrast, a comprehensive study by Alquist, Kilian, and Vigfusson (2011) finds that neither the nominal nor the real price of oil follows a random walk. This said, while at short time horizons reduced-form autoregressive and vector autoregressive models of the global oil market are found to be more accurate than the random walk forecast of the real price of oil, these gains diminish quickly as time horizons lengthen. Beyond one or two years, the no-change forecast of the real price of oil is the predictor with the lowest mean-square prediction error. Also, the authors find no reliable evidence that oil futures prices or professional and government forecasts significantly lower the mean square prediction error relative to the no-change forecast at short horizons; and long-term futures prices are distinctly less accurate than the no-change forecast.

In addition, as discussed earlier, resource revenue largely originates from abroad, and hence affects the domestic economy differently from nonresource tax revenues. Moreover, total GDP can be very volatile since it reflects changes in resource prices through the resource GDP deflator.

Another approach to estimate the SB that avoids the problems just discussed is to focus on the *structural nonresource primary balance (NRPB) as a share of nonresource GDP (NRGDP)*. The structural NRPB is the NRPB adjusted for the influence of the nonresource cycle and nonstructural elements. This method of assessing the cyclically adjusted fiscal stance of countries heavily dependent on resource revenue avoids the problems just discussed. It abstracts from resource revenue, avoids attempts at estimating "structural" resource revenue, and refrains from using total GDP as the scaling factor.

Villafuerte, López-Murphy, and Ossowski (2010), for example, assess the cyclicality of fiscal policy in Latin American resource-rich countries using this methodology. They first estimate the nonresource economic cycle by quantifying the nonresource output gap (NROG), applying a standard Hodrick-Prescott filter to the time series of NRGDP in real terms. The NROG is defined as the actual NRGDP minus estimated trend NRGDP as a share of trend NRGDP. Second, the NRPB is broken down as the sum of the cyclically adjusted NRPB and the cyclical NRPB, assuming, in common with much of the literature, a nonresource revenue elasticity of 1 and an expenditure elasticity of 0 with respect to the NROG. Finally, the cyclicality of fiscal policy is assessed by examining the link between changes in the NROG and changes in the cyclically adjusted NRPB.

The estimation of CABs and SBs is a complex exercise fraught with uncertainty in all countries, and even more so in resource-rich countries. It requires a well-developed statistical base and significant technical capacity (Ter-Minassian 2010). There are different approaches used for the estimation of potential output and output gaps (such as filtering and production function techniques) and of revenue and expenditure elasticities to the cycle. All the methodologies used have limitations.

There are a number of other indicators that can be used to help gauge whether the economy suffers from overheating besides estimates of the NROG. Macroeconomic and sectoral indicators can help frame short-run nonresource fiscal policies. In particular, policy makers can focus their attention on the following indicators: (i) rising inflation rates[3]; (ii) a significantly higher rate of growth of domestic demand than the rate of growth of NRGDP; (iii) labor shortages that force employers to raise wages in excess of estimated labor productivity gains; (iv) supply constraints in the construction sector and ancillary industries and rising construction costs, indicative of excessive pressures stemming from investment demand in the private and public sectors; (v) indicators of capacity utilization above historical averages, and the exhaustion of spare resources; (vi) large capital inflows; and (vii) significant increases in bank lending to the private sector.

Notes

1. Expenditures may also be adjusted for the cycle, particularly in countries where they are sensitive to the cycle, for example, if significant unemployment compensation schemes are in place.

2. In one example of the effect of the estimation uncertainty, Izquierdo and Talvi (2008) and Vladkova-Hollar and Zettelmeyer (2008) arrived at different conclusions about the fiscal stance of Latin American countries in the 2000s, mainly because of differences in their assumptions about the persistence of resource price changes.

3. For example, during the 2003–08 oil boom, inflation rose markedly in a number of oil-exporting countries (OECs). The higher inflation also reflected the strong increase in international food prices over the period.

Chile's Structural Balance Fiscal Guideline

Since 2001 fiscal policy in Chile has been built on the concept of a central government structural balance (SB). It has been supported by a fiscal guideline targeting that balance.

Estimated "structural" budget revenues are those that would be achieved if the economy were operating at full potential and the prices of copper and molybdenum were at their "long-term" levels. Two independent panels of experts estimate potential output and the "long-term" metal prices. Their inputs are used in the budget process. The fiscal guideline allows full operation of automatic stabilizers from the budget's revenue side.

Compliance with the SB targets is not legally binding. The guideline acts mainly as a self-imposed and self-assessed constraint by the government. This said, successive governments have reiterated their commitment to the guideline, have announced fiscal targets for the duration of their mandates, and have mostly complied with them. The 2006 Fiscal Responsibility Law institutionalized key aspects of the framework and introduced two resource funds.

The SB guideline has been subject to methodological changes and refinements since 2005, which increased its computational complexity and arguably reduced transparency (IMF 2010b). The fiscal target was eased several times since 2008. In 2009 the target was reduced in the midst of the global financial crisis and the decline in metal prices, and was defined to exclude the impact of temporary nonmining tax reduction measures, which allowed a more expansionary fiscal policy. In 2010 the guideline was temporarily suspended following a massive earthquake. Following the crisis, the government announced its objective to reduce the structural deficit to 1 percent of gross domestic product (GDP) by 2014; in the event, the structural deficits in 2012 and 2013 already beat that target. The government has recently set a target of a balanced structural fiscal position by 2018.

In 2010 the government established an expert commission to review the fiscal guideline and suggest improvements. The commission issued a number of recommendations (Chile, Comité Asesor 2011), which included:

- Complementing the guideline with a mechanism giving the government authority to implement countercyclical fiscal policies.
- Not giving special treatment to temporary tax reductions when computing cyclical adjustments, except for tax measures with automatic sunset clauses; the SB should reflect adjustments to fiscal revenues only to the extent that they are affected by the economic cycle and by deviations of metal prices from their estimated structural levels.
- Introducing exit clauses for exceptional circumstances together with the specification of the policies to return to the fiscal target.
- Not making cyclical adjustments for interest income or interest payments.
- Transitioning to a primary balance indicator in the future.
- Strengthening transparency, including the provision of more information to the public.
- Establishing an independent fiscal council.

Most of the recommendations have been adopted by the government.[1] A fiscal council was set by decree in 2013 to advise the ministry of finance (MoF) on the implementation and operation of the fiscal guideline and methodological changes. A draft law currently before Congress aims at giving the council a stronger legal basis.

The fiscal guideline has been a cornerstone of Chile's strong economic performance. The guideline arguably helped the government deflect spending pressures when metal prices surged in the 2000s and build up significant liquidity buffers which were partly used when the need arose in the 2009 downturn.

The success of the guideline is seen to have been mainly due to a number of factors: policy credibility; political commitment; a strong institutional framework, including significant fiscal powers vested in the executive branch[2]; broad social consensus; the independence of the expert committees that ensures that the underlying economic assessment is separate from other considerations in the budget-preparation process, which enhances credibility; and an effective inflation-targeting mechanism.

This said, some technical issues merit closer analysis. This concerns mainly long-term copper price estimates and the technical design of the guideline.

Long-term copper price. It is not clear whether copper has a well-defined long-run average price, as discussed above.[3] Hence, the interpretation of the "long-term" copper price estimated by the expert committee (which, it should be clarified, does not correspond to market futures prices) is unclear.

Potential procyclicality of the fiscal guideline. The structural (overall) balance is not necessarily a good indicator of the impact of fiscal policy on domestic demand (see appendix B; Dabán 2011; IMF 2012f). The framework can give rise to unintended procyclicality of fiscal policy.

Consider a simple example, where the expert committee raises the estimated long-term copper price from one year to the next. This raises estimated structural copper revenues and hence allows an increase in government expenditure that might, objectively, be procyclical, given the cyclical position of the nonresource economy. But the measured SB would remain unchanged, and therefore the procyclicality of fiscal policy would not be picked up by the chosen targeted fiscal indicator.

In fact, the expert committee's estimation of the "long-term" price of copper has not been independent from the international copper price cycle. The committee's views were influenced by the positive copper price shock in the 2000s: the committee gradually increased the estimated long-term copper price over time as international copper prices surged. Hence, the increase in the price of copper imparted procyclicality to fiscal policy indirectly through the structural copper price estimates of the expert committee (IMF 2010b).

And indeed, during the copper boom, both in 2006 and 2008 the *structural nonresource primary deficit* estimated by the International Monetary Fund (IMF)—which, the IMF notes, is a better indicator of the direction of fiscal policy and its economic effects than the change in the overall SB—increased, even though the estimated output gap was positive and rising (IMF 2010b, 2012f). This gave rise to IMF-estimated procyclical fiscal impulses of 1¼ percent and 2¾ percent of GDP respectively, in those years, which were not picked up by the targeted fiscal indicator.

Notes

1. Based on the findings of the expert commission, the government revised upward the estimated structural deficits in 2009–10. The revised deficits were higher than the targets in the fiscal guideline.

2. Only the executive branch may take fiscal initiatives. The legislature can only approve or reject them. In particular, the legislature may not change the budgeted revenues or increase expenditures.

3. The expert commission acknowledged the methodological difficulties in estimating a "long-term" copper price.

APPENDIX D

Direct Distribution of Resource Rents to Citizens

In recent years a number of researchers and commentators have proposed the direct distribution of revenues to the citizens or the residents of resource-rich countries, as cash transfers. Proposals differ in terms of how much to distribute, what distribution mechanisms should be used, and who the recipients should be.[1]

A key thread running through these proposals is the observation that in a number of resource-rich countries, resource revenue has been associated with poor economic performance, itself the result in large measure of poor institutional quality associated with the ready availability of resource rents. Revenues have often been mismanaged, have not contributed to development, and have given rise to waste, corruption, rent capture, patronage, and clientelism.

Many proponents of direct distribution tend to view widespread governance problems, lack of transparency, and corruption as almost intractable in terms of the remedies usually recommended. In their view, the political economy of rent distribution is a formidable barrier against progress in transparency, governance, and accountability and better economic management. What incentives would there be for any part of government to increase transparency and accountability in revenue management, if increased transparency would reduce the opportunities for rent seeking and raise its expected cost? Given the powerful vested interests that would be affected, they doubt that governments would implement reform agendas aimed at improving governance and transparency and improving public financial management (PFM) and the quality of spending. Direct distribution is viewed as a radical measure that strikes at the heart of the problem and delivers other benefits as well.

A second and related strand of arguments put forth for direct distribution, is that individuals are better at managing resources and investing, than are corrupt governments. Finally, direct distribution targeted particularly at the poor, has been seen as a potentially powerful mechanism that could raise the incomes of poor people.

Several key arguments are made:

Direct distribution would transform the resource-rich country into a "nonresource" economy where taxes build accountability. If governments could not get hold of the resource rents directly, but instead had to raise revenue by taxing these rents after they had been distributed to the citizens, they would be no different from countries without natural resources. Resources available for patronage, corruption, and rent capture would be withdrawn or at least subject to greater scrutiny. Once "easy money" is eliminated, much of the problem would go away. The need for governments to tax would, unlike spending manna from heaven, increase accountability and public monitoring of how resources are used—and to build tax administration capacity.

Individuals are better at taking spending and investment decisions, and have stronger incentives to do it well than do ineffective resource-rich country governments. Giving money to individuals would remove credit constraints often present in low-income resource-rich countries and allow them to invest in worthwhile undertakings (Venables 2011).

Direct distribution would support equity and would be good for low-income people. Transfers would be progressive, and would involve a more pro-poor policy than government spending in resource-rich countries (Moss 2011). Transfers would also be a mechanism for formalization and inclusion (Rodríguez, Morales, and Monaldi 2012). It has been estimated that in countries such as Angola, Equatorial Guinea, and Gabon, about a tenth of the resource revenue currently accruing to the government, would be enough to raise the income of every poor person up to the national poverty line (Giugale and Nguyen 2014). In Nigeria, achieving the same results would take up a fifth of oil revenue. It should be noted that these estimates were made prior to the fall in oil prices that started in the second half of 2014.

Governments considering direct distribution, however, should give thought to a number of issues. These will be more or less relevant depending on the size of the distribution program considered and specific country circumstances.

The transfers distributed could quickly be seen as an entitlement. The experience of Alaska's permanent dividend program, suggests that such transfers are quickly perceived as entitlements.[2] If at a later stage changes in the dividend program are needed (for example, at a time of sustained revenue penury, or because resources are needed for other pressing objectives, or because resource revenue declines as resources are depleted), proposals to reduce transfers could be strongly opposed. Depending on the size of the transfer program, this could compromise fiscal sustainability.

Provision of public goods and externalities. Will government resources after distribution suffice to finance an adequate provision of public goods and investment spending in physical and human capital with positive externalities—externalities that transfer recipients will not internalize in their private spending decisions? Against this argument it has been noted that in resource-rich countries where governments have used resource revenues to finance poor quality spending, waste, and corruption, direct distribution may not necessarily reduce the provision of public services—rather, it might reduce waste (Giugale 2015).

Intergenerational equity. Nonrenewable resources are exhaustible. But a significant share of the transfers might end up being consumed. Would the interest of future generations be safeguarded if the revenues were distributed to the current generation?

Limited implementation capacity and weak transfer systems. Running an effective, efficient, and transparent direct distribution program with adequate governance assurances could pose challenges to the PFM systems of countries with poor institutional capacity and governance issues. In countries plagued by corruption, transfer systems are no exception, and direct distribution programs could become a source of patronage and illicit payments as much as any other flow of public funds, though perhaps in some cases distribution could be outsourced.

Taxation. In low-income resource-rich countries where personal income tax systems are often weak, it is not clear whether there would be capacity to tax the transfers. In countries characterized by corruption, tax systems are not exempt, and tax evasion is greatly facilitated by corruption.

Reducing distributions at a time of falling revenues could face opposition due to concerns about social impact. When revenues are falling or are projected to be "low," there could be popular and political resistance to cutting distributions back, and/or calls to supplement them with other cash transfers to reduce the impact on households, with fiscal implications. Of course, reductions in government spending in traditional expenditure systems can also face strong opposition—this is not a feature of distribution per se, but opposition could be particularly strong if transfers are an important component of household income.

Direct distribution could transmit resource revenue volatility and uncertainty to the domestic economy. As discussed in chapter 2, there are strong macroeconomic reasons to smooth government expenditure. Resource revenue is volatile, so distributions could be volatile and uncertain, in principle going up and down with resource revenues. Thus, distribution could transmit volatility and uncertainty to households, who, particularly in the absence of well-functioning credit markets, may not be well equipped to handle it.[3] It could also be procyclical: transfers would be high when the private sector is likely to be doing well, and low when the economy is in recession. Depending on the size of the distribution program, this could result in boom-and-bust episodes damaging to growth.

It should be noted that using smoothing mechanisms for distributions, such as backward-looking moving-average formulas, would reduce household income volatility and uncertainty. At a time of rising resource prices, however, this mechanism would leave part of the resource revenue with the government, which it could use in a procyclical manner for other purposes with the promise that the distribution "fund" will be replenished later. This could be a time-inconsistent commitment: at a time of falling resource prices, will the government distribute more than current revenues, as entailed by smoothing schemes, if it does not have adequate financial buffers?

Direct distribution could affect labor supply. Distribution could increase dependence on state handouts and reduce the incentives to engage in productive work. This will depend on the size of the transfers.

Notes

1. For example, see Sala-i-Martín and Subramanian (2003), Sandbu (2006), Segal (2011), Moss (2011), Devarajan and others (2011), Rodríguez, Morales, and Monaldi (2012), and Giugale and Nguyen (2014). Gupta, Segura-Ubiergo, and Flores (2014) provide a survey of the issues and international experience and offer a preliminary assessment.

2. Referring to Alaska's permanent dividend program, Goldsmith (2004) has commented that "[a]ny politician who even suggests considering a policy that might adversely impact the size of the annual distribution had best look for another career." In a 2003 poll 64 percent of Alaskans believed that they were entitled to a dividend check even if had a budget deficit (Lewis 2004).

3. Indeed, a key argument for the centralization of resource revenue in federal systems is that the central government is better equipped to deal with volatility and risk than are subnational governments (SNGs).

Generally Accepted Principles and Practices of a Sovereign Wealth Fund: The Santiago Principles

Generally Accepted Principle and Practice (GAPP) 1[1]
The legal framework for the sovereign wealth fund (SWF) should be sound and support its effective operation and the achievement of its stated objective(s).

- *GAPP 1.1 Subprinciple.* The legal framework for the SWF should ensure the legal soundness of the SWF and its transactions.
- *GAPP 1.2 Subprinciple.* The key features of the SWF's legal basis and structure, as well as the legal relationship between the SWF and the other state bodies, should be publicly disclosed.

GAPP 2
The policy purpose of the SWF should be clearly defined and publicly disclosed.

GAPP 3
Where the SWF's activities have significant direct domestic macroeconomic implications, those activities should be closely coordinated with the domestic fiscal and monetary authorities, so as to ensure consistency with the overall macroeconomic policies.

GAPP 4
There should be clear and publicly disclosed policies, rules, procedures, or arrangements in relation to the SWF's general approach to funding, withdrawal, and spending operations.

- *GAPP 4.1 Subprinciple.* The source of SWF funding should be publicly disclosed.
- *GAPP 4.2 Subprinciple.* The general approach to withdrawals from the SWF and spending on behalf of the government should be publicly disclosed.

GAPP 5

The relevant statistical data pertaining to the SWF should be reported on a timely basis to the owner, or as otherwise required, for inclusion where appropriate in macroeconomic data sets.

GAPP 6

The governance framework for the SWF should be sound, and establish a clear and effective division of roles and responsibilities, in order to facilitate accountability and operational independence in the management of the SWF, to pursue its objectives.

GAPP 7

The owner should set the objectives of the SWF, appoint the members of its governing body(ies) in accordance with clearly defined procedures, and exercise oversight over the SWF's operations.

GAPP 8

The governing body(ies) should act in the best interests of the SWF, and have a clear mandate and adequate authority and competency to carry out its functions.

GAPP 9

The operational management of the SWF should implement the SWF's strategies in an independent manner and in accordance with clearly defined responsibilities.

GAPP 10

The accountability framework for the SWF's operations should be clearly defined in the relevant legislation, charter, other constitutive documents, or management agreement.

GAPP 11

An annual report and accompanying financial statements of the SWF's operations and performance should be prepared in a timely fashion and in accordance with recognized international or national accounting standards in a consistent manner.

GAPP 12

The SWF's operations and financial statements should be audited annually in accordance with recognized international or national auditing standards in a consistent manner.

GAPP 13

Professional and ethical standards should be clearly defined and made known to members of the SWF's governing body(ies), management, and staff.

GAPP 14

Dealing with third parties for the purpose of the SWF's operational management should be based on economic and financial grounds, and follow clear rules and procedures.

GAPP 15
SWF operations and activities in host countries should be conducted in compliance with all applicable regulatory and disclosure requirements of the countries in which they operate.

GAPP 16
The governance framework and objectives, as well as the manner in which the SWF's management is operationally independent from the owner, should be publicly disclosed.

GAPP 17
Relevant financial information regarding the SWF should be publicly disclosed to demonstrate its economic and financial orientation, so as to contribute to stability in international financial markets and enhance trust in recipient countries.

GAPP 18
The SWF's investment policy should be clear and consistent with its defined objectives, risk tolerance, and investment strategy, as set by the owner or the governing body(ies), and be based on sound portfolio management principles.

- *GAPP 18.1 Subprinciple.* The investment policy should guide the SWF's financial risk exposures and the possible use of leverage.
- *GAPP 18.2 Subprinciple.* The investment policy should address the extent to which internal and/or external investment managers are used, the range of their activities and authority, and the process by which they are selected and their performance monitored.
- *GAPP 18.3 Subprinciple.* A description of the investment policy of the SWF should be publicly disclosed.

GAPP 19
The SWF's investment decisions should aim to maximize risk-adjusted financial returns in a manner consistent with its investment policy, and based on economic and financial grounds.

- *GAPP 19.1 Subprinciple.* If investment decisions are subject to other than economic and financial considerations, these should be clearly set out in the investment policy and be publicly disclosed.
- *GAPP 19.2 Subprinciple.* The management of an SWF's assets should be consistent with what is generally accepted as sound asset management principles.

GAPP 20
The SWF should not seek or take advantage of privileged information or inappropriate influence by the broader government in competing with private entities.

GAPP 21

SWFs view shareholder ownership rights as a fundamental element of their equity investments' value. If an SWF chooses to exercise its ownership rights, it should do so in a manner that is consistent with its investment policy and protects the financial value of its investments. The SWF should publicly disclose its general approach to voting securities of listed entities, including the key factors guiding its exercise of ownership rights.

GAPP 22

The SWF should have a framework that identifies, assesses, and manages the risks of its operations.

- *GAPP 22.1 Subprinciple.* The risk management framework should include reliable information and timely reporting systems, which should enable the adequate monitoring and management of relevant risks within acceptable parameters and levels, control and incentive mechanisms, codes of conduct, business continuity planning, and an independent audit function.
- *GAPP 22.2 Subprinciple.* The general approach to the SWF's risk management framework should be publicly disclosed.

GAPP 23

The assets and investment performance (absolute and relative to benchmarks, if any) of the SWF should be measured and reported to the owner according to clearly defined principles or standards.

GAPP 24

A process of regular review of the implementation of the GAPP should be engaged in by or on behalf of the SWF.

Note

1. This appendix is based on IWGS (2008).

The International Monetary Fund's Guide to Resource Revenue Transparency: Summary of Good Fiscal Transparency Practices for Resource Revenue Management

Clarity of Roles and Responsibilities[1]

Legal Framework for Resource Revenues

The government's ownership of resources in the ground should be clearly established in law, and the power to grant rights to explore, produce, and sell these resources should be well established in laws, regulations, and procedures that cover all stages of resource development.

Fiscal Regime

The government's policy framework and legal basis for taxation or production-sharing agreements with resource companies should be presented to the public clearly and comprehensively.

Authority over Revenue Flows and Borrowing

Fiscal authority over resource-related revenue and borrowing is clearly specified in the law. Legislation should require full disclosure of all resource-related revenue, loan receipts and liabilities, and asset holdings.

Equity Participation

Government involvement in the resource sector through equity participation should be fully disclosed and the implications explained to the public.

National Resource Companies

Ownership structures of national resource companies and their fiscal role vis-à-vis the resource sector ministry and the finance ministry should be clearly defined.

Commercial responsibilities should be clearly distinguished from policy, regulatory, and social obligations.

Quasi-Fiscal Activities of Resource Companies

Arrangements whereby international or national resource companies undertake social or environmental expenditure or provide subsidies to producers or consumers without explicit budget support, should be clearly defined and described in the budget documentation.

Subnational Government and Resource Revenues

Arrangements to assign or share resource revenue between central and subnational levels of government should be well defined and explicitly reflect national fiscal policy and macroeconomic objectives.

Open Budget Processes

Fiscal Policy and Resource Revenues

The budget framework should incorporate a clear policy statement on the rate of exploitation of natural resources and the management of resource revenues, referring to the government's overall fiscal and economic objectives, including long-term fiscal sustainability.

Fiscal Policy, Resource-Related Funds, and the Budget

Mechanisms for coordinating the operations of any funds established for resource revenue management with other fiscal activities should be clearly specified.

Operations of Resource-Related Funds

Operational rules applied to resource-related funds should be clearly stated as part of an overall fiscal policy framework.

Fiscal Policy and Asset Management

The investment policies for assets accumulated through resource revenue savings should be clearly stated, including through a statement in the annual budget documents.

Accounting for Resource Revenues

The government accounting system or special fund arrangements should clearly identify all government resource revenue receipts and enable issuance of timely, comprehensive, and regular reports to the public, ideally as part of a comprehensive budget execution report. The reports should be based on a clear statement of the accounting basis (cash or accrual) and policies.

Public Availability of Information

Budget Documentation of Resource Revenues and Spending
All resource-revenue-related transactions, including through resource funds, should be clearly identified, described, and reported in the budget process and final accounts documents.

Reporting on Company Resource Revenue Payments
Reports on government receipts of company resource revenue payments should be made publicly available as part of the government budget and accounting process.

Fiscal Balance
The (primary) nonresource fiscal balance should be presented in budget documents as an indicator of the macroeconomic impact and sustainability of fiscal policy, in addition to the overall balance and other relevant fiscal indicators.

Reporting on Resource-Related Debt
The government's published debt reports should identify any direct or indirect collateralization of future resource production, for instance, through precommitment of production to lenders. All government contractual risks and obligations arising from such debt should be disclosed.

Reporting on Assets
All financial assets held by government domestically or abroad, including those arising from resource-related activities, should be fully disclosed in government financial statements.

Estimating Resource Asset Worth
Estimates of resource asset worth based on probable production streams and assumptions should be disclosed.

Reporting Contingent Liabilities and Quasi-Fiscal Activities
Government contingent liabilities and the cost of resource company quasi-fiscal activities arising from resource-related contracts, should be reported in budget accounts or other relevant documents, in a format that helps assess fiscal risks and the full extent of fiscal activity.

Fiscal Risks
Risks associated with resource revenue, particularly price risks and contingent liabilities, should be explicitly considered in annual budget documents, and measures taken to address them should be explained, and their performance monitored.

Assurances of Integrity

Internal Control and Audit of Resource Revenues

Internal control and audit procedures for handling resource revenue receipts through government accounts or special fund arrangements, and any spending of such receipts through special funds, should be clearly described and disclosed to the public.

Tax Administration Openness

Tax administration should be conducted to ensure that resource companies understand their obligations, entitlements, and rights. The scope for discretionary action by tax officials should be clearly defined in laws and regulations, and the adequacy of sector skills and standard or sector-specific procedures should be open to review.

Oversight of Companies

International and national resource companies should comply fully with internationally accepted standards for accounting, auditing, and publication of accounts.

Oversight of Company/Government Revenue Flows

A national audit office or other independent organization should report regularly to the legislature on the revenue flows between international and national companies and the government and on any discrepancies between different sets of data on these flows.

Note

1. This appendix is based on IMF (2007a).

References

Acemoğlu, D., and J. Robinson. 2006. "Economic Backwardness in Political Perspective." *American Political Science Review* 100 (February): 115–31.

Aghion, P., and A. Banerjee. 2005. *Volatility and Growth.* Oxford and New York: Oxford University Press.

Ahmad, E., and G. Brosio, eds. 2006. *Handbook of Fiscal Federalism.* Cheltenham: Edward Elgar Publishing Limited.

———. 2015. *Handbook of Multilevel Finance.* Cheltenham: Edward Elgar Publishing Limited.

Ahmad, E., and E. Mottu. 2003. "Oil Revenue Assignments: Country Experiences and Issues." In *Fiscal Policy Formulation and Implementation in Oil-Producing Countries,* edited by J. M. Davis, R. Ossowski, and A. Fedelino. Washington, DC: International Monetary Fund (IMF).

Aizenman, J., and N. Marion. 1999. "Volatility and Investment: Interpreting Evidence from Developing Countries." *Economica* 66 (262): 157–79.

Aizenman, J., and B. Pinto. 2005. *Managing Volatility and Crises.* New York: Cambridge University Press.

Akitoby, B., and S. Coorey, eds. 2012. *Oil Wealth in Central Africa: Policies for Inclusive Growth.* Washington, DC: IMF.

Al-Hassan, A., M. Papaioannou, M. Skancke, and C. Sung. 2013. "Sovereign Wealth Funds: Aspects of Governance Structures and Investment Management." IMF Working Paper WP/13/231, International Monetary Fund, Washington, DC.

Alberola, E., and J. M. Montero. 2006. "Debt Sustainability and Procyclical Fiscal Policies in Latin America." Working Paper 0611, Bank of Spain, Madrid.

Albino-War, M., S. Cerovic, F. Grigoli, J. Flores, J. Kapsoli, H. Qu, Y. Said, B. Shukurov, M. Sommer, and S. Yoon. 2014. "Making the Most of Public Investment in MENA and CCA Oil-Exporting Countries." IMF Staff Discussion Note SDN/14/10, International Monetary Fund, Washington, DC.

Alexeev, M., and R. Conrad. 2009. "The Elusive Curse of Oil." *The Review of Economics and Statistics* 91 (3): 589–98.

Alier, M. Undated. "Measuring Budget Rigidities in Latin America." Unpublished.

Allen, R. 2013. "Managing Extrabudgetary Funds." In *The International Handbook of Public Financial Management,* edited by R. Hemming, R. Allen, and B. Potter. London: Palgrave Macmillan.

Allen, R., and S. Vani. 2013. "Financial Management and Oversight of State-Owned Enterprises." In *The International Handbook of Public Financial Management*, edited by R. Hemming, R. Allen, and B. Potter. London: Palgrave McMillan.

Alquist, R., L. Kilian, and R. Vigfusson. 2011. "Forecasting the Price of Oil." International Finance Discussion Paper No. 1022, Board of Governors of the Federal Reserve System, Washington, DC.

Amuzegar, J. 2005. "Iran's Oil Stabilization Fund: A Misnomer." *Middle East Economic Survey* XLVIII (47). http://www.payvand.com/news/05/nov/1221.html.

Anderson, G., ed. 2012. *Oil and Gas in Federal Systems*. Don Mills, ON: Oxford University Press.

Arezki, R., and K. Ismail. 2010. "Boom-Bust Cycle, Asymmetrical Fiscal Response and the Dutch Disease." IMF Working Paper WP/10/94, International Monetary Fund, Washington, DC.

Auty, R. 2001. *Resource Abundance and Economic Development*. New York: World Institute for Development Economics Research and Oxford University Press.

Auty, R., and R. Mikesell. 1998. *Sustainable Development in Mineral Economies*. New York: Oxford University Press.

Bacon, R., and S. Tordo. 2006. *Experiences with Oil Funds: Institutional and Financial Aspects*. Technical Report 321/06, ESMAP, World Bank, Washington, DC.

Barma, N., K. Kaiser, T. M. Le, and L. Viñuela. 2012. *Rents to Riches? The Political Economy of Natural Resource-Led Development*. Washington, DC: World Bank.

Barnett, S., and R. Ossowski. 2003. "Operational Aspects of Fiscal Policy in Oil-Producing Countries." In *Fiscal Policy Formulation and Implementation in Oil-Producing Countries*, edited by J. M. Davis, R. Ossowski, and A. Fedelino. Washington, DC: IMF.

Bartsch, U. 2006. "How Much is Enough? Monte Carlo Simulations of an Oil Stabilization Fund for Nigeria." IMF Working Paper WP/06/142, International Monetary Fund, Washington, DC.

Baunsgaard, T., and S. Symansky. 2009. "Automatic Fiscal Stabilizers." IMF Staff Position Note SPN/09/23, International Monetary Fund, Washington, DC.

Baunsgaard, T., M. Villafuerte, M. Poplawski-Ribeiro, and C. Richmond. 2012. "Fiscal Frameworks for Resource Rich Developing Countries." IMF Staff Discussion Note SDN/12/04, International Monetary Fund, Washington, DC.

Berg, A., R. Portillo, S. Yang, and L. Zanna. 2012. "Public Investment in Resource Abundant Developing Countries." IMF Working Paper WP/12/274, International Monetary Fund, Washington, DC.

Bleaney, M., and H. Halland. 2014. "Natural Resource Exports, Fiscal Policy Volatility and Growth." *Scottish Journal of Political Economy* 61 (5): 502–22.

———. 2016. "Do Resource-Rich Countries Suffer from a Lack of Fiscal Discipline?" World Bank Policy Working Paper 7552, World Bank, Washington, DC.

Bornhorst, F., G. Dobresen, A. Fedelino, J. Gottschalk, and T. Nakata. 2011. "When and How to Adjust Beyond the Business Cycle? A Guide to Structural Fiscal Balances." IMF Technical Notes and Manuals TNM/11/02, International Monetary Fund, Washington, DC.

Bourguignon, F., and T. Verdier. 2000. "Oligarchy, Democracy, Inequality, and Growth." *Journal of Development Economics* 62: 285–313.

Bova, E., N. Carcenac, and M. Guerguil. 2014. "Fiscal Rules and the Procyclicality of Fiscal Policy in the Developing World." IMF Working Paper WP/14/122, International Monetary Fund, Washington, DC.

Bova, E., P. Medas and T. Poghosyan. 2016. "Macroeconomic Stability in Resource Rich Countries: The Role of Fiscal Policy." IMF Working Paper WP/16/36, International Monetary Fund, Washington, DC.

BP. 2015. *Statistical Review of World Energy June 2015*. London: BP.

Brahmbhatt, M., and O. Canuto. 2010. "Natural Resources and Development Strategy after the Crisis." *Economic Premise* 71 (February). https://openknowledge.worldbank.org/bitstream/handle/10986/10212/531640BRI0Econ10Box345599B01PUBLIC1.pdf?sequence=1.

Brosio, G. 2003. "Oil Revenue and Fiscal Federalism." In *Fiscal Policy Formulation and Implementation in Oil-Producing Countries*, edited by J. M. Davis, R. Ossowski, and A. Fedelino. Washington, DC: IMF.

Brumby, J., and R. Hemming. 2013. "Medium-Term Expenditure Frameworks." In *The International Handbook of Public Financial Management*, edited by R. Hemming, R. Allen, and B. Potter. London: Palgrave Macmillan.

Brunnschweiler, C., and E. Bulte. 2006. "The Resource Curse Revisited and Revised: A Tale of Paradoxes and Red Herrings." CER-ETH Economics Working Paper Series 06/61, Center of Economic Research, ETH Zurich. https://ideas.repec.org/p/eth/wpswif/06-61.html.

Calder, J. 2014. *Administering Fiscal Regimes for the Extractive Industries: A Handbook*. Washington, DC: IMF. http://www.elibrary.imf.org/doc/IMF071/20884-9781475575170/20884-9781475575170/Other_formats/Source_PDF/20884-9781484386446.pdf.

Calderón, C., and L. Servén. 2014. "Infrastructure, Growth, and Inequality: An Overview." Policy Research Working Paper 7034, Development Research Group, Macroeconomics and Growth Team, World Bank, Washington, DC.

Carreón-Rodríguez, V., and J. Rosellón. 2012. "Mexico." In *Oil and Gas in Federal Systems*, edited by G. Anderson. Don Mills, ON: Oxford University Press.

Carstens, A. 2005. "The Role of Transparency and Accountability for Economic Development in Resource Rich Countries." Address at the Regional Workshop on Transparency and Accountability in Resource Management in CEMAC Countries, Malabo, Equatorial Guinea, January 27, 2005.

Cebotari, A. 2008. "Contingent Liabilities: Issues and Practice." IMF Working Paper WP/08/245, International Monetary Fund, Washington, DC.

Cebotari, A., L. Lusinyan, A. Mati, P. Mauro, M. Petrie, and R. Velloso. 2009. *Fiscal Risks: Sources, Disclosure and Management*. IMF Fiscal Affairs Department. Washington, DC: IMF.

Celasun, O., X. Debrun, and J. Ostry. 2006. "Primary Surplus Behavior and Risks to Fiscal Sustainability in Emerging Market Countries: A 'Fan Chart' Approach." IMF Working Paper WP/06/182, International Monetary Fund, Washington, DC.

Cetrángolo, O., and J. P. Jiménez, eds. 2009. *Rigideces y Espacios Fiscales en América Latina*. Santiago de Chile: Economic Commission for Latin America and the Caribbean (CEPAL).

Chile, Comité Asesor. 2011. *Propuestas para Perfeccionar la Regla Fiscal*. Comité Asesor para el Diseño de una Política Fiscal de Balance Estructural de Segunda Generación para Chile. Santiago: Dirección de Presupuesto, Ministerio de Hacienda.

Clark, P., and A. Monk. 2015. "Sovereign Development Funds: Designing High-Performance, Strategic Investment Institutions." http://www.top1000funds.com/wp-content/uploads/2015/10/SDFs-Designing-High-Performance-Strategic-Investment-Institutions.pdf.

Clemente, L., R. Faris, and A. Puente. 2002. "Dependencia de los Recursos Naturales, Volatilidad y Desempeño Económico en Venezuela: El Papel de un Fondo de Estabilización." In *Proyecto Andino de Competitividad*. Caracas: Corporación Andina de Fomento.

Collier, P. 2012. "Savings and Investment Decisions in Resource-Rich Low-Income Countries." In *Commodity Price Volatility and Inclusive Growth in Low-Income Countries*, edited by R. Arezki, C. Pattillo, M. Quintyn, and M. Zhu. Washington, DC: IMF.

Collier, P., and A. Hoeffler. 2004. "Greed and Grievance in Civil War." *Oxford Economic Papers* 56: 563–95.

Collier, P., F. van der Ploeg, M. Spence, and A. J. Venables. 2009. "Managing Resource Revenues in Developing Economies." OxCarre Working Papers, Oxford Centre for the Analysis of Resource Rich Economies, Oxford.

Colombia. 2013. *Marco Macro-Fiscal de Mediano Plazo 2013*. Bogotá: Ministerio de Hacienda y Crédito Público.

Corbacho, A., and T. Ter-Minassian. 2013. "Public Financial Management Requirements for Effective Implementation of Fiscal Rules." In *The International Handbook of Public Financial Management*, edited by R. Hemming, R. Allen, and B. Potter. London: Palgrave Macmillan.

Corden, M., and P. Neary. 1982. "Booming Sector and De-Industrialisation in a Small Open Economy." *The Economic Journal* 92 (December): 825–48.

Cordes, T., T. Kinda, P. Muthoora, and A. Weber. 2015. "Expenditure Rules: Sound Tools for Fiscal Policy?" IMF Working Paper WP/15/29, International Monetary Fund, Washington, DC.

Crain, W., and J. Devlin. 2003. *Nonrenewable Resource Funds: A Red Herring for Fiscal Stability?* Fairfax and Washington, DC: George Mason University and World Bank.

Cueva, S. 2008. "Ecuador: Fiscal Stabilization Funds and Prospects." Country Department Andean Group Working Paper CSI-110, Inter-American Development Bank (IDB), Washington, DC.

Cuevas, A. 2003. "Reforming Intergovernmental Relations in Argentina." IMF Working Paper WP/03/90, International Monetary Fund, Washington, DC.

Dabán, T. 2011. "Strengthening Chile's Rule-Based Fiscal Framework." IMF Working Paper WP/11/17, International Monetary Fund, Washington, DC.

Dabán, T., and J. L. Hélis. 2010. "A Public Financial Management Framework for Resource-Producing Countries." IMF Working Paper WP/10/72, International Monetary Fund, Washington, DC.

Dabán, T., and J. L. Hélis. 2013. "Public Financial Management in Natural Resource-Rich Countries." In *Public Financial Management and Its Emerging Architecture*, edited by M. Cangiano, T. Curristine and M. Lazare. Washington, DC: IMF.

Dabla-Norris, E., and E. Paul. 2006. "What Transparency Can Do When Incentives Fail: An Analysis of Rent Capture." IMF Working Paper WP/06/146, International Monetary Fund, Washington, DC.

Dabla-Norris, E., J. Brumby, A. Kyobe, Z. Mills, and C. Papageorgiu. 2011. "Investing in Public Investment: An Index of Public Investment Efficiency." IMF Working Paper WP/11/37, International Monetary Fund, Washington, DC.

Dabla-Norris, E., R. Allen, L. Zanna, T. Prakash, E. Kvintradze, V. Lledo, I. Yackovlev, and S. Gollwitxer. 2010. "Budget Institutions and Fiscal Performance in Low-Income Countries." IMF Working Paper WP/10/80, International Monetary Fund, Washington, DC.

Daniel, P., M. Keen, and C. McPherson. 2010. *The Taxation of Petroleum and Minerals: Principles, Problems, and Practice*. Abingdon and Washington, DC: Routledge and IMF.

Darby, S., and K. Lempa. 2007. "Advancing the EITI in the Mining Sector: Implementation Issues." Paper produced by the World Bank's Oil, Gas, and Mining Policy and Operations Unit, World Bank, Washington, DC.

Das, U., A. Mazarei, and H. van der Hoorn, eds. 2010. *Economics of Sovereign Wealth Funds*. Washington, DC: IMF.

Davis, G., and J. Tilton. 2005. "The Resource Curse." *Natural Resources Forum* 29 (3): 233–42. http://lawweb.colorado.edu/profiles/syllabi/banks/Davis%2520%2520 Tilton%2520-%2520The%2520resource%2520curse.pdf.

Davis, J., R. Ossowski, and A. Fedelino, eds. 2003. *Fiscal Policy Formulation and Implementation in Oil-Producing Countries*. Washington, DC: IMF.

Davis, J., R. Ossowski, J. Daniel, and S. Barnett. 2003. "Stabilization and Savings Funds for Nonrenewable Resources: Experience and Fiscal Policy Implications." In *Fiscal Policy Formulation and Implementation in Oil-Producing Countries*, edited by J. Davis, R. Ossowski, and A. Fedelino. Washington, DC: IMF.

De Renzio, P., and J. Wehner. 2015. "The Impacts of Fiscal Openness: A Review of the Evidence." Global Initiative for Fiscal Transparency and International Budget Partnership.

Deutsche Bank. 2014. "EM Oil Producers: Breakeven Pain Thresholds." http://etf. deutscheawm.com/DEU/DEU/Download/Research-Global/2dd759fe-b80a-4f07-a51c-dd02f4d384e5/EM-oil-producers-breakeven-pain.pdf.

Devarajan, S., H. Ehrhart, T. Le, and G. Raballand. 2011. "Direct Redistribution, Taxation, and Accountability in Oil-Rich Economies: A Proposal." Working Paper 281, Center for Global Development, Washington, DC.

Devlin, J., and M. Lewin. 2005. "Managing Oil Booms and Busts in Developing Countries." In *Managing Economic Volatility and Crisis*, edited by J. Aizenman, and B. Pinto. New York: Cambridge University Press.

Easterly, W., T. Irwin, and L. Servén. 2008. "Walking Up the Down Escalator: Public Investment and Fiscal Stability." *World Bank Research Observer* 23 (1): 37–56.

Echeverry, J. C., V. Navas, and A. Clavijo. 2009. "Rigideces Presupuestales en Colombia y el Perú." In *Rigideces y Espacios Fiscales en América Latina*, edited by O. Cetrángolo, and J. P. Jiménez. Santiago de Chile: CEPAL.

Eckardt, S., I. Sarsenov, and M. R. Thomas. 2012. "The Fiscal Management of Natural Resource Revenues in a Developing Country Setting (or How to Design a Fiscal Rule if You are Not Norway)." Poverty Reduction and Economic Management Note No. 164, World Bank, Washington, DC, April 2012.

Eifert, B., A. Gelb, and N. B. Tallroth. 2003. "The Political Economy of Fiscal Policy and Economic Management in Oil-Exporting Countries." In *Fiscal Policy Formulation and Implementation in Oil-Producing Countries*, edited by J. M. Davis, R. Ossowski, and A. Fedelino. Washington, DC: IMF.

Engel, E., and R. Valdés. 2000. "Optimal Fiscal Strategy for Oil Exporting Countries." IMF Working Paper WP/00/118, International Monetary Fund, Washington, DC.

Engel, E., C. Neilsen, and R. Valdés. 2010. "Chile's Structural Balance Rule as Social Policy." Presentation at the Banco Central de Chile Conference on "Fiscal Policy and Macroeconomic Performance," October 22, 2010, Banco Central de Chile, Santiago.

Escolano, J. 2010. "A Practical Guide to Public Debt Dynamics, Fiscal Sustainability, and Cyclical Adjustment of Budget Aggregates." IMF Technical Notes and Manuals TNM/10/02, International Monetary Fund, Washington, DC.

Estache, A., and R. Liu. 2003. "Social Rates of Return on World Bank Infrastructure Projects: A Review of 40 Years Experiment." PowerPoint Presentation, World Bank, Washington, DC (cited in World Bank 2006b).

Everaert, G., M. Fouad, E. Martin, and R. Velloso. 2009. "Disclosing Fiscal Risks in the Post-Crisis World." IMF Staff Position Note SPN/09/18, International Monetary Fund, Washington, DC.

Fainboim, I. 2009. "Changing the Financial Management of the Defense Sector in Chile: Leaving Expenditure Earmarking Behind." IMF PFM Blog, November 25, 2009. http://blog-pfm-imf.org/pfmblog/2009/11/posted-by-israel-fainboim.html.

Fatás, A., and I. Mihov. 2003. "The Case for Restricting Fiscal Policy Discretion." *The Quarterly Journal of Economics* 118 (4): 1419–47.

———. 2005. "Policy Volatility, Institutions, and Economic Growth." CEPR Discussion Paper No. 5388, Centre for Economic Policy Research, London.

Financial Times. 2000. "Chávez 'Misused' Oil Windfall Revenue." March 24, 2000.

Foster, V., and C. Briceño-Garmendia. 2010. *Africa's Infrastructure: A Time for Transformation.* Washington, DC: World Bank.

Frankel, J. 2010. "The Natural Resource Curse: A Survey." NBER Working Paper 15836, National Bureau of Economic Research, Cambridge, MA.

———. 2011. "How Can Commodity Exporters Make Fiscal and Monetary Policy Less Procyclical?" Faculty Research Working Paper No. 11–015, Harvard Kennedy School, Cambridge, Massachusetts.

Gabon. 2012. "Décret du Création du FGIS." http://www.fgis-gabon.com/?page_id=1118.

Gelb, A. 2002. "Economic and Export Diversification in Mineral Countries." Presentation to the World Bank Managing Volatility Thematic Group on Best Practice in Diversification Strategies for Mineral Exporting Countries, January 7, 2002, Washington, DC.

Gelb, A., and S. Garsmann. 2010. "How Should Oil Exporters Spend their Rents?" Working Paper 221, Center for Global Development, Washington, DC.

Gelb, A., S. Tordo, and H. Halland. 2014. "Sovereign Wealth Funds and Long-Term Development Finance." Policy Research Working Paper 6776, Poverty Reduction and Economic Management Network, Public Sector Governance Unit, and Sustainable Development Network, Oil, Gas, and Mining Unit, World Bank, Washington, DC.

Ghana. 2011. *Petroleum Revenue Management Act.* Accra: Ministry of Finance.

———. 2013. *2013 Annual Report on the Petroleum Funds.* Accra: Ministry of Finance.

———. 2014. *2014 Annual Report on the Petroleum Funds.* Accra: Ministry of Finance.

———. 2015. *Petroleum Revenue Management (Amendment Bill).* Accra: Parliament of Ghana.

Giugale, M. 2015. "Cheap Oil and the Poor." http://www.huffingtonpost.com/marcelo-giugale/cheap-oil-and-the-poor_b_6443150.html.

Giugale, M., and N. Nguyen. 2014. "Money to the People: Estimates of the Potential Scale of Direct Dividend Payments in Africa." Policy Paper 043, Center for Global Development, Washington, DC.

Glenday, G. 2013. "Revenue Forecasting." In *The International Handbook of Public Financial Management*, edited by R. Hemming, R. Allen, and B. Potter. London: Palgrave Macmillan.

Goldsmith, S. 2004. "The Alaska Permanent Fund Dividend: An Experiment in Wealth Distribution." In *Promoting Income Security as a Right: Europe and North America*, edited by G. Standing. London: Anthem.

Gupta, S., A. Segura-Ubiergo, and E. Flores. 2014. "Direct Distribution of Resource Revenues: Worth Considering?" IMF Staff Discussion Note SDN/14/05, International Monetary Fund, Washington, DC.

Gupta, S., A. Kangur, C. Papageorgiou, and A. Wane. 2014. "Efficiency Adjusted Public Capital and Growth." *World Development* 57: 164–78.

Gust, C., and D. Zakharova. 2012. "Strengthening Russia's Fiscal Framework." IMF Working Paper WP/12/76, International Monetary Fund, Washington, DC.

Gylfason, T., T. Herbertsson, and G. Zoega. 1999. "A Mixed Blessing: Natural Resources and Economic Growth." *Macroeconomic Dynamics* 3: 205–25.

Halland, H., M. Lokanc, and A. Nair. 2015. *The Extractive Industries Sector: Essentials for Economists, Public Finance Professionals, and Policy Makers*. World Bank Studies Series. Washington, DC: World Bank.

Halland, H., M. Noel, and S. Tordo. Forthcoming 2016. "Strategic Investment Funds: Seizing the Opportunities and Managing the Challenges." Policy Research Working Paper Series, World Bank, Washington, DC.

Hamilton, J. 2008. "Understanding Crude Oil Prices." Department of Economics Working Paper, University of California, San Diego.

Hamilton, K., and E. Ley. 2010. "Measuring National Income and Growth in Resource-Rich, Income Poor Countries." *Economic Premise* 28 (August). http://siteresources.worldbank.org/INTPREMNET/Resources/EP28.pdf.

Heald, D. 2013. "Strengthening Fiscal Transparency." In *The International Handbook of Public Financial Management*, edited by R. Hemming, R. Allen, and B. Potter . London: Palgrave Macmillan.

Heilbrunn, J. 2002. "Governance and Oil Funds." Mimeo, World Bank, Washington, DC.

Hemming, R. 2013a. "The Macroeconomic Framework for Managing Public Finances." In *The International Handbook of Public Financial Management*, edited by R. Hemming, R. Allen, and B. Potter. London: Palgrave Macmillan.

———. 2013b. "The Role of Independent Fiscal Agencies." In *The International Handbook of Public Financial Management*, edited by R. Hemming, R. Allen, and B. Potter. London: Palgrave Macmillan.

Hemming, R., and P. Joyce. 2013. "The Role of Fiscal Councils in Promoting Fiscal Discipline and Sound Government Finances." In *Public Financial Management and its Emerging Architecture*, edited by M. Cangiano, T. Curristine, and M. Lazare. Washington, DC: IMF.

Heuty, A., and J. Aristi. 2010. *Fool's Gold: Assessing the Performance of Alternative Fiscal Instruments During the Commodities Boom and the Global Crisis.* New York: Revenue Watch Institute.

Hnatkovska, V., and N. Loayza. 2005. "Volatility and Growth." In *Managing Volatility and Crises,* edited by J. Aizenman, and B. Pinto. New York: Cambridge University Press.

Husain, A., K. Tazhibayeva, and A. Ter-Martirosyan. 2008. "Fiscal Policy and Economic Cycles in Oil-Exporting Countries." IMF Working Paper WP/08/253, International Monetary Fund, Washington, DC.

IMF (International Monetary Fund). 2003. *Ecuador: Article IV Consultation, Request for Stand-By Arrangement and Approval of an Exchange Restriction.* IMF Country Report 03/90. Washington, DC: IMF.

———. 2004. *Gabon: 2003 Article IV Consultation and Staff Monitored Program.* IMF Country Report 04/28. Washington, DC: IMF.

———. 2005a. *Republic of Equatorial Guinea: Report on the Observance of Standards and Codes-Fiscal Transparency Module.* IMF Country Report 05/144. Washington, DC: IMF.

———. 2005b. *Algeria: 2005 Article IV Consultation.* IMF Country Report 05/93. Washington, DC: IMF.

———. 2005c. *Gabon: Selected Issues and Statistical Appendix.* IMF Country Report 05/47. Washington, DC: IMF.

———. 2005d. *Mexico: Article IV Consultation.* IMF Country Report 05/427. Washington, DC: IMF.

———. 2006a. *Ecuador: Selected Issues.* IMF Country Report 06/103. Washington, DC: IMF.

———. 2006b. *Regional Economic Outlook, Western Hemisphere.* Washington, DC: IMF.

———. 2007a. *Guide on Resource Revenue Transparency.* Washington, DC: IMF.

———. 2007b. *Chad: Selected Issues and Statistical Appendix.* IMF Country Report 07/28. Washington, DC: IMF.

———. 2008. *Regional Economic Outlook, Middle East, and Central Asia.* Washington, DC: IMF.

———. 2009a. *Fiscal Rules—Anchoring Expectations for Sustainable Public Finances.* Washington, DC: IMF.

———. 2009b. *Norway: Report on Observance of Standards and Codes—Fiscal Transparency Module.* Washington, DC: IMF.

———. 2010a. *Managing Natural Resource Wealth Topical Trust Fund: Program Document.* Washington, DC: IMF.

———. 2010b. *Chile: 2010 Article IV Consultation.* IMF Country Report 10/298. Washington, DC: IMF.

———. 2011a. *Islamic Republic of Iran: 2011 Article IV Consultation.* IMF Country Report 11/241. Washington, DC: IMF.

———. 2011b. *Botswana: 2011 Article IV Consultation.* IMF Country Report 11/248. Washington, DC: IMF.

———. 2012a. *Macroeconomic Policy Frameworks for Resource Rich Developing Countries.* Washington, DC: IMF.

———. 2012b. *Republic of Congo: 2012 Article IV Consultation.* IMF Country Report 12/283. Washington, DC: IMF.

———. 2012c. *Fiscal Regimes for Extractive Industries: Design and Implementation.* Washington, DC: IMF.

———. 2012d. *Botswana: Article IV Consultation.* IMF Country Report 12/234. Washington, DC: IMF.

———. 2012e. *Global Financial Stability Report* (April 2012). Washington, DC: IMF.

———. 2012f. *Chile: Article IV Consultation.* IMF Country Report 12/267. Washington, DC: IMF.

———. 2013a. *Regional Economic Outlook: Middle East and Central Asia.* Washington, DC: IMF.

———. 2013b. *Gabon: 2012 Article IV Consultation.* IMF Country Report 13/55. Washington, DC: IMF.

———. 2013c. *Mexico: Selected Issues.* IMF Country Report 13/133. Washington, DC: IMF.

———. 2013d. "Revised Guidelines for Foreign Exchange Reserve Management." IMF Policy Paper, International Monetary Fund, Washington, DC.

———. 2013e. *Nigeria: 2012 Article IV Consultation.* IMF Country Report 13/116. Washington, DC: IMF.

———. 2014a. *Mongolia: 2013 Article IV Consultation.* IMF Country Report 14/64. Washington, DC: IMF.

———. 2014b. *Norway: 2014 Article IV Consultation.* IMF Country Report 14/259. Washington, DC: IMF.

———. 2014c. *Islamic Republic of Iran: Selected Issues Paper.* IMF Country Report 14/94. Washington, DC: IMF.

———. 2014d. *Islamic Republic of Iran: 2014 Article IV Consultation.* IMF Country Report 14/93. Washington, DC: IMF.

———. 2014e. *Angola: Second Post-Program Monitoring.* IMF Country Report 14/81. Washington, DC: IMF.

———. 2014f. *Angola: Selected Issues Paper.* IMF Country Report 14/275. Washington, DC: IMF.

———. 2014g. *Angola: 2014 Article IV Consultation.* IMF Country Report 14/274. Washington, DC: IMF.

———. 2014h. *Sovereign Asset-Liability Management—Guidance for Resource-Rich Economies.* Washington, DC: IMF.

———. 2014i. *Template to Collect Data on Government Revenues from Natural Resources.* Washington, DC: IMF.

———. 2014j. *Republic of Congo: 2014 Article IV Consultation.* IMF Country Report 14/72. Washington, DC: IMF.

———. 2015a. *Fiscal Monitor,* October 2015. Washington, DC: IMF.

———. 2015b. *Regional Economic Outlook Update: Middle East and Central Asia Department.* Washington, DC: IMF.

———. 2015c. *Ghana: Request for Three-Year Arrangement Under the Extended Credit Facility.* IMF Country Report 15/103. Washington, DC: IMF.

———. 2015d. *Mongolia: 2015 Article IV Consultation.* IMF Country Report 15/109. Washington, DC: IMF.

———. 2015e. *Gabon: 2014 Article IV Consultation*. IMF Country Report 15/47. Washington, DC: IMF.

IMF and World Bank. 2001. *Macroeconomic Policy and Poverty Reduction*. Washington, DC: IMF and World Bank.

———. 2011. *Managing Volatility in Low-Income Countries: The Role and Potential for Contingent Financial Instruments*. Washington, DC: IMF and World Bank.

———. 2012. *Revisiting the Debt Sustainability Framework for Low-Income Countries*. Washington, DC: IMF and World Bank.

Irwin, T. 2012. "Accounting Devices and Fiscal Illusions." IMF Staff Discussion Note SDN/12/02, International Monetary Fund, Washington, DC.

Isham, J., M. Woolcock, L. Pritchett, and G. Busby. 2005. "The Varieties of Resource Experience: Natural Resource Export Structures and the Political Economy of Economic Growth." *World Bank Economic Review* 19 (2): 141–74.

IWGS (International Working Group of Sovereign Wealth Funds). 2008. "Sovereign Wealth Funds: Generally Accepted Principles and Practices: Santiago Principles." http://www.ifswf.org.

Izquierdo, A., and E. Talvi. 2008. *All that Glitters May Not Be Gold: Assessing Latin America's Recent Macroeconomic Performance*. Washington, DC: IDB.

Kose, M., E. Prasad, and M. Terrones. 2005. "Growth and Volatility in an Era of Globalization." *IMF Staff Papers* 52: 31–63.

Kraay, A., and L. Servén. 2013. "Fiscal Policy as a Tool for Stabilization in Developing Countries." Background Note for the *2014 World Development Report*, World Bank, Washington, DC.

Kumar, M., and T. Ter-Minassian. 2007. *Promoting Fiscal Discipline*. Washington, DC: IMF.

Lange, G. 2004. "Wealth, Natural Capital, and Sustainable Development: Contrasting Examples from Botswana and Namibia." *Environmental and Resource Economics* 29 (3): 257–83.

Laursen, T., and S. Mahajan. 2005. "Volatility, Income Distribution, and Poverty." In *Managing Volatility and Crises*, edited by J. Aizenman and B. Pinto. New York: Cambridge University Press.

Lewis, T. 2004. "Devoted to the Dividend: Budget Crisis or Not, Alaskans Love Getting Their Share of Oil Wealth." *Alaska Magazine*, September. Anchorage: Alaska Publishing Properties Inc.

Ley, E. 2010. "Exhaustible Resources and Fiscal Policy: Copper Mining in Zambia." Paper prepared as background for the Public Expenditure Review, World Bank, Washington, DC.

Loayza, N., R. Ranciere, L. Servén, and J. Ventura. 2007. "Macroeconomic Volatility and Welfare in Developing Countries: An Introduction." *World Bank Economic Review* 21 (3): 343–57.

Manzano, O., F. Monaldi, J. M. Puente, and S. Vitale. 2012. "Venezuela." In *Oil and Gas in Federal Systems*, edited by G. Anderson. Don Mills, ON: Oxford University Press.

Matsuyama, K. 1992. "Agricultural Productivity, Comparative Advantage, and Economic Growth." *Journal of Economic Theory* 58: 317–443.

Medas, P., and D. Zakharova. 2009. "A Primer on Fiscal Analysis in Oil-Producing Countries." IMF Working Paper WP/09/56, International Monetary Fund, Washington, DC.

Megginson, W. and V. Fotak. 2016. "Rise of the Fiduciary State: A Survey of Sovereign Wealth Fund Research." In *A Collection of Surveys on Savings and Wealth Accumulation*, edited by E. Claus and I. Claus. Chichester: Blackwell Wiley.

Mehlum, H., K. Moene, and R. Torvik. 2006. "Institutions and the Resource Curse." *The Economic Journal* 116 (January): 1–20.

Moser, G., S. Rogers, and R. van Til. 1997. "Nigeria: Experience with Structural Adjustment." Occasional Paper 148, International Monetary Fund, Washington, DC.

Moss, T. 2011. "Oil to Cash: Fighting the Resource Curse through Cash Transfers." Working Paper 237, Center for Global Development, Washington, DC.

Natural Resource Governance Institute. 2014. "Natural Resource Funds: Managing the Public Trust: How to Make Natural Resource Funds Work for Citizens." New York: Natural Resource Governance Institute and Columbia Center on Sustainable International Investment.

Nigeria. 2014. *2014–16 Medium-Term Expenditure Framework and Fiscal Strategy Paper*. Abuja: Budget Office of the Federation.

Norway. 2001. *Report No. 29 to the Storting (2000–2001): Guidelines for Economic Policy*. Oslo: Ministry of Finance.

———. 2013. *Long-Term Perspectives for the Norwegian Economy 2013—A Summary*. Meld. St. 12 (2012–13) Report to the Storting (White Paper) Summary. Oslo: Ministry of Finance.

OECD (Organisation for Economic Co-operation and Development). 2004. *OECD Principles of Corporate Governance*. Paris: OECD.

———. 2006. *OECD Guidelines on Corporate Governance of State-Owned Enterprises*. Paris: OECD.

OECD and IDB (Inter-American Development Bank). 2014. *Government at a Glance: Latin America and the Caribbean 2014: Towards Innovative Public Financial Management*. Paris: OECD.

Ossowski, R. 2013a. "Fiscal Rules and Resource Funds in Nonrenewable Resource Exporting Countries: International Experience." Discussion Paper IDB/DP/290, Inter-American Development Bank, Washington, DC.

———. 2013b. "Managing Non-Renewable Resource Revenues." In *The International Handbook of Public Financial Management*, edited by R. Hemming, R. Allen, and B. Potter. London: Palgrave Macmillan.

Ossowski, R., M. Villafuerte, P. Medas, and T. Thomas. 2008. "Managing the Oil Revenue Boom: The Role of Fiscal Institutions." Occasional Paper 260, International Monetary Fund, Washington, DC.

Peru. 2014. *Marco Macroeconómico Multianual 2015–17*. Lima: Ministerio de Economía y Finanzas.

Petersen, C., and N. Budina. 2003. *Governance Framework of Oil Funds: The Case of Azerbaijan and Kazakhstan*. Washington, DC: World Bank.

Petrie, M. 2013. "Managing Fiscal Risk." In *The International Handbook of Public Financial Management*, edited by R. Hemming, R. Allen, and B. Potter. London: Palgrave McMillan.

Pinto, B. 1987. "Nigeria During and After the Oil Boom: A Policy Comparison with Indonesia." *World Bank Economic Review* I (3): 419–45.

Rajaram, A. 2012. "Improving Public Investment Efficiency: Transforming Natural Resource Revenues into Development Assets." Presentation at the Conference on Management of Natural Resources in Sub-Saharan Africa, Kinshasa, March 21–22, 2012. http://www.imf.org/external/np/seminars/eng/2012/Kinshasa/pdf/ar.pdf.

Rajaram, A., T. M. Le, N. Bletska, and J. Brumby. 2010. "A Diagnostic Framework for Assessing Public Investment Management." Policy Research Working Paper 5397, Africa Region Public Sector Reform and Capacity Building Unit and Poverty Reduction and Economic Management Network, Public Sector Unit, World Bank, Washington, DC.

Rajaram, A., T. M. Le, K. Kaiser, J. Kim, and J. Frank, eds. 2014. *The Power of Public Investment Management: Transforming Resources into Assets for Growth*. Washington, DC: World Bank.

Ramey, G., and V. Ramey. 1995. "Cross-Country Evidence on the Link Between Volatility and Growth." *American Economic Review* 85 (5) (December 1995): 1138–51.

Rodríguez, P., J. Morales, and F. Monaldi. 2012. "Direct Distribution of Oil Revenues in Venezuela: A Viable Alternative?" Working Paper 306, Center for Global Development, Washington, DC.

Ross, M., K. Kaiser, and N. Mazaheri. 2011. "The 'Resource Curse' in MENA? Political Transitions, Resource Wealth, Economic Shocks, and Conflict Risk." Policy Research Working Paper 5742, Poverty Reduction and Economic Management Network, Public Sector Governance Unit, World Bank, Washington, DC.

Ruiz, J. 2010. "Earmarking in Central American Countries." IMF PFM Blog, December 28, 2010. http://blog-pfm-imf.org/pfmblog/2010/12/earmarking-in-central-american-countries.html.

Sachs, J., and A. Warner. 1995. "Natural Resource Abundance and Economic Growth." NBER Working Paper 5398, National Bureau of Economic Research, Cambridge, MA.

São Tomé and Principe. 2004. *National Assembly: Law No. 8/2004 Oil Revenue Law*. São Tomé.

Sala-i-Martin, X., and A. Subramanian. 2003. "Addressing the Natural Resource Curse: An Illustration from Nigeria." Working Paper 9804, National Bureau of Economic Research, Cambridge, MA.

Sandbu, M. 2006. "Natural Wealth Accounts: A Proposal for Alleviating the Natural Resource Curse." *World Development* 34 (7): 1153–70.

Schaechter, A., T. Kinda, N. Budina, and A. Weber. 2012. "Fiscal Rules in Response to the Crisis—Toward the 'Next Generation' Rules. A New Dataset." IMF Working Paper WP12/187, International Monetary Fund, Washington, DC.

Schiavo-Campo, S. 2007. *Toward a Medium-Term Expenditure Framework (MTEF)*. Washington, DC: World Bank. http://www.siteresources.worldbank.org/PSGLP/Resources/MTEFsSchiavoCampo.pdf.

Segal, P. 2011. "Resource Rents, Redistribution, and Halving Global Poverty: The Resource Dividend." *World Development* 39 (4): 475–1489.

Servén, L. 2007. "Fiscal Rules, Public Investment, and Growth." Policy Research Working Paper 4382, Development Research Group, Macroeconomics and Growth Team, World Bank, Washington, DC.

Shabsigh, G., and N. Ilahi. 2007. "Looking Beyond the Fiscal: Do Oil Funds Bring Macroeconomic Stability?" IMF Working Paper WP/07/96, International Monetary Fund, Washington, DC.

Shah, A., ed. 2007. *Budgeting and Budgetary Institutions*. Washington, DC: World Bank.

Sharma, N., and T. Strauss. 2013. *Special Fiscal Institutions for Resource-Rich Developing Economies*. London: Overseas Development Institute.

Shields, J. 2013. "Sovereign Wealth Funds." In *The International Handbook of Public Financial Management*, ed. R. Hemming, R. Allen, and B. Potter. London: Palgrave Macmillan.

Shields, J., and M. Villafuerte. 2010. "Sovereign Wealth Funds and Economic Policy at Home." In *Economics of Sovereign Wealth Funds*, edited by U. Das, A. Mazarei, and H. van der Hoorn. Washington, DC: IMF.

Sinnott, E., J. Nash, and A. de la Torre. 2010. *Natural Resources in Latin America and the Caribbean: Beyond Booms and Busts?* Washington, DC: World Bank.

Skancke, M. 2003. "Fiscal Policy and Petroleum Fund Management in Norway." In *Fiscal Policy Formulation and Implementation in Oil-Producing Countries*, edited by J. M. Davis, R. Ossowski, and A. Fedelino. Washington, DC: IMF.

Smith, P. 1991. "The Politics of Plenty: Investing Natural Resource Revenues in Alberta and Alaska." *Canadian Public Policy-Analyse de Politiques* XVII (2): 139–54.

Sturm, M., F. Gurtner, and J. González Alegre. 2009. "Fiscal Policy Challenges in Oil-Exporting Countries." Occasional Paper 104, European Central Bank, Frankfurt.

Sugawara, N. 2014. "From Volatility to Stability in Expenditure: Stabilization Funds in Resource-Rich Countries." IMF Working Paper WP/14/43, International Monetary Fund, Washington, DC.

Takizawa, J., E. Gardner, and K. Ueda. 2004. "Are Developing Countries Better Off Spending Their Oil Wealth Upfront?" IMF Working Paper WP/04/141, International Monetary Fund, Washington, DC.

Talvi, E., and C. Végh. 2005. "Tax Base Variability and Procyclical Fiscal Policy in Developing Countries." *Journal of Development Economics*, Elsevier 78 (1): 156–90.

Ter-Minassian, T. 1997. *Fiscal Federalism in Theory and Practice*. Washington, DC: IMF.

———. 2010. "Preconditions for the Successful Introduction of Structural Fiscal Balance-Based Rules in Latin America and the Caribbean: A Framework Paper." Discussion Paper IDB-DP-157, Inter-American Development Bank, Washington, DC.

———. 2012. "Structural Reforms in Brazil: Progress and Unfinished Agenda." IDB Policy Brief No. IDB-PB-158, Inter-American Development Bank, Washington, DC.

Timor-Leste. 2005. *Petroleum Fund Law*. Dili: Ministry of Finance.

———. 2014. *República Democrática de Timor Leste: State Budget 2014-Budget Overview, Book 1*. Dili: Ministry of Finance.

Tornell, A., and P. Lane. 1999. "The Voracity Effect." *American Economic Review* 89 (1): 22–46.

Torvik, R. 2001. "Learning by Doing and the Dutch Disease." *European Economic Review* 45: 285–306. http://www.sv.ntnu.no/iso/Ragnar.Torvik/science.pdf.

———. 2002. "Natural Resources, Rent Seeking, and Welfare." *Journal of Development Economics* 67: 455–70.

UNCTAD (United Nations Conference on Trade and Development). 2013. "Time Series on Inward and Outward Foreign Direct Investment Flows, Annual, 1970–2012." Data compiled by the *Financial Times*, August 19, 2013, "Offshore Centres Race to Seal Africa Investment Tax Deals." http://www.ft.com/intl/cms/s/0/64368e44-08c8-11e3-ad07-00144feabdc0.html.

Van der Ploeg, F. 2011. "Natural Resources: Curse or Blessing?" *Journal of Economic Literature* 49 (2): 366–420.

———. 2012. "Bottlenecks in Ramping Up Public Investment." *International Tax and Public Finance* 19 (4): 509–38.

Van der Ploeg, F., and A. Venables. 2008. "Harnessing Windfall Revenues in Developing Economies: Sovereign Wealth Funds and Optimal Tradeoffs between Citizen Dividends, Public Infrastructure, and Debt Reduction." CEPR Discussion Paper No. 6954, Centre for Economic Policy Research, London.

Van der Ploeg, F., and S. Poelhekke. 2010. "The Pungent Smell of 'Red Herrings': Subsoil Assets, Rents, Volatility, and the Resource Curse." *Journal of Environmental Economics and Management* 60: 44–55.

Venables, A. 2011. "Resource Revenue Management." Paper written for the Asian Development Bank's Knowledge Sharing Platform for Resource Revenue Management, Manila, April 2011, Centre for the Analysis of Resource Rich Economies, Department of Economics, Oxford University, Oxford.

Villafuerte, M., and P. López-Murphy. 2010. "Fiscal Policy in Oil Producing Countries during the Recent Oil Price Cycle." IMF Working Paper WP/10/28, International Monetary Fund, Washington, DC.

Villafuerte, M., P. López-Murphy, and R. Ossowski. 2010. "Riding the Roller Coaster: Fiscal Policies of Nonrenewable Resource Exporters in Latin America and the Caribbean." IMF Working Paper WP/10/251, International Monetary Fund, Washington, DC.

Vladkova-Hollar, I., and J. Zettelmeyer. 2008. "Fiscal Positions in Latin America: Have They Really Improved?" IMF Working Paper 08/137, International Monetary Fund, Washington, DC.

Warrack, A., and R. Keddie. Undated. "Alberta Heritage Fund vs. Alaska Permanent Fund: A Comparative Analysis." Faculty of Business, University of Alberta, Edmonton, Canada.

Watson, A. 2011. "International Experience Oil and Gas Budget Revenue Management." Presentation at the Expert Meeting, Resource Taxation in Russia, May 12–13, 2011.

World Bank. 1998. *Public Expenditure Management Handbook*. Washington, DC: World Bank.

———. 2006a. *Where is the Wealth of Nations?* Washington, DC: World Bank.

———. 2006b. "Fiscal Policy for Growth and Development: An Interim Report." Background Paper (DC2006-003) for April 2006 Meeting of the Development Committee, World Bank Group and International Monetary Fund, Washington, DC.

———. 2007. "Fiscal Policy for Growth and Development: Further Analysis and Lessons from Country Case Studies." Background Paper (DC2007-0004) for April 2007 Meeting of the Development Committee, World Bank Group and International Monetary Fund, Washington, DC.

———. 2010a. *Lao PDR Development Report 2010: Natural Resource Management for Sustainable Development*. Washington, DC: World Bank.

———. 2010b. *Public Financial Management Reform in the Middle East and North Africa: An Overview of Regional Experience. Part II: Individual Country Cases*. Middle East and North Africa Vice-Presidency. Washington, DC: World Bank.

————. 2011. *The Changing Wealth of Nations*. Washington, DC: World Bank.

————. 2012. *Beyond the Annual Budget: Global Experience with Medium Term Expenditure Frameworks*. Washington, DC: World Bank.

————. 2013a. "Beyond Oil: Kazakhstan's Path to Greater Prosperity Through Diversifying." Poverty Reduction and Economic Management Unit, Europe and Central Asia Region, World Bank, Washington, DC.

————. 2013b. *Country Partnership Strategy for the Democratic Republic of Timor Leste for the Period FY 2013-FY 2017*. Washington, DC: World Bank.

————. 2014a. "Generating Sustainable Wealth from Mozambique's Natural Resource Boom." World Bank Mozambique Policy Note, World Bank, Washington, DC.

————. 2014b. "Mongolia Economic Update, December 2014." World Bank Group in Mongolia.

Yépez-García, R., and J. Dana. 2012. *Mitigating Vulnerability to High and Volatile Oil Prices: Power Sector Experience in Latin America and the Caribbean*. Washington, DC: World Bank.

York, R., and Z. Zhan. 2009. "Fiscal Vulnerability and Sustainability in Oil-Producing Sub-Saharan African Countries." IMF Working Paper 09/174, International Monetary Fund, Washington, DC.

ECO-AUDIT

Environmental Benefits Statement

The World Bank Group is committed to reducing its environmental footprint. In support of this commitment, the Publishing and Knowledge Division leverages electronic publishing options and print-on-demand technology, which is located in regional hubs worldwide. Together, these initiatives enable print runs to be lowered and shipping distances decreased, resulting in reduced paper consumption, chemical use, greenhouse gas emissions, and waste.

The Publishing and Knowledge Division follows the recommended standards for paper use set by the Green Press Initiative. The majority of our books are printed on Forest Stewardship Council (FSC)–certified paper, with nearly all containing 50–100 percent recycled content. The recycled fiber in our book paper is either unbleached or bleached using totally chlorine free (TCF), processed chlorine free (PCF), or enhanced elemental chlorine free (EECF) processes.

More information about the Bank's environmental philosophy can be found at http://crinfo.worldbank.org/wbcrinfo/node/4.